IS THERE MORE TO LIFE THAN LIVING?

Discovering L.I.F.E.

KEN MILES

Praise for
Is There More to Life than Living?

You gotta read this book! Ken Miles launches us on an adventure of discovering four simple and yet profoundly practical Biblical truths. These insights will not only help you grow spiritually but will enable you to make a difference in the lives of the people around you. I found myself constantly challenged to self examination all the while excited to begin to put into practice what I was learning.

– Ken Taylor,
Lead Pastor Creekside Church

Should you want to really connect with God and enjoy a life of truly authentic faith then "Is There More to Life Than Living?" by my good friend Ken Miles is the book for you. The carefully chosen stories, quotes and illustrations make it an easy read but the practical and inspiring content will help you live a deeply meaningful and even joy-filled life. The four pillars of the book: Love; Integrity; Forgiveness and Excellence will strengthen your faith and refresh your soul for years to come.

- David Macfarlane,
Billy Graham Organization

The message of the gospel is about how it can transform a life. It is not simply about a nice message but actually brings us into a relationship with the author of life. In his book, "Is there More to Life than Living?" Ken Miles, a pastor and friend for many years, shares with us some insight that has helped many to embrace the practical aspects of living the Life of Christ. Though the principles are not new, his acronym of L.I.F.E. and the balancing of Love, Integrity, Forgiveness, and Excellence is presented in an interesting and fresh way that helps draw the reader into desiring the fruit of the life God has for each of us. I would encourage you to read this book with an open heart and allow God to speak to you about your own life.

- Pastor Steve Fleming,
Koinonia Christian Fellowship

Ken Miles has always been a very gifted speaker. But now in writing this book, he has opened the door of his inner life and shown us yet another of his many God-given talents. With wonderful insights and crystal clear illustrations, Ken reveals to us the amazing adventure of our new life in Christ. Enjoy this book but, more importantly learn from it.

- Fred Morris, Centre Wellington town councilor and founder of Vision Financial

I have benefitted from Ken Miles' objective balance and wisdom many times in our long friendship. He always speaks the truth in love. In his new book Ken answers the hard ques-

tions we ask when we are searching for the abundant life that Christ has promised. Discover L.I.F.E. principles and you will have a roadmap for a life well lived.

*- Paul Cowell,
President of Christian Hospitality Network*

Ken Miles has distilled four decades of successful ministry into one word. You won't be able to see the word 'LIFE' again without the enriching contents of this book coming to mind!

*- Jim Gordon,
Lead Pastor Elora Road Christian Fellowship*

IS THERE MORE TO LIFE THAN LIVING?
Copyright ©2016 by Ken Miles.

All rights reserved.

All Scripture quotations, unless otherwise indicated, are taken from the New King James Version. Copyright ©1982 by Thomas Nelson Inc.

ISBN 978-0-9940592-6-0

Published by Joshua Gordon BookWorks
www.joshuagordonbookworks.com

To Kay, the love of my life

Table of Contents

Introduction 13

CHAPTER 1: There Is More Than One Kind of Life 17

CHAPTER 2: The Facets of God's Life in You 29

CHAPTER 3: Making God Visible 37

CHAPTER 4: Love - the Impossible Commandment 45

CHAPTER 5: Integrity - Honesty with God and Others ... 77

CHAPTER 6: Forgiveness - Without Qualifiers 121

CHAPTER 7: Excellence - a Godly Process 159

CHAPTER 8: Living out your New L.I.F.E. 205

Is There More to Life Than Living?

Introduction

Is that all there is?
Is that all there is?
If that's all there is my friends
Then let's keep dancing
Let's break out the booze and have a ball
If that's all there is.
- Song Lyrics of "Is That All There Is"

One of my favorite stories is about three vagabonds who had spent much time together panhandling in the streets. One of them was given a lottery ticket by a kind-hearted passerby, which to his great delight won the million-dollar jackpot. With unbridled enthusiasm, the new millionaire indulged himself in every destructive habit and vice which his new found wealth could afford. Unfortunately, his health could not withstand the strain and he died shortly thereafter. However, before he died, he gave instructions for a most unusual burial. When the day arrived his two buddies were in attendance at the cemetery. What they observed was an extraordinary sight. Their friend had paid handsomely for the funeral home to bury him propped up behind the steering wheel of a brand new Cadillac. As the crane lowered the shiny vehicle into the over-sized grave, his pals saw their friend dressed in a brand new suit with a cigar stuck between his lips. As the sun sparkled off the diamond ring on his finger and gleamed in the eye of one of his buddies, he turned to his friend and said, "Man, now that's what I call living."

I like this story because it illustrates so well that we can be deceived into thinking that "really living" is indulging ourselves, acquiring things and impressing others. Yet, many who have accomplished these things have discovered that they still feel lifeless on the inside. Others may look on thinking that the person's accomplishments and possessions have brought them fulfillment and try to duplicate them. Sadly, they don't realize that by following this example they will end up in the same dark hole because of the absence of life on the inside.

What do you call living?

We all have a natural physical life that we share in common. It allows us to exist. But is there more to life than existing? Why do we all have a hunger for something more? Modern culture has expressed this desire in many ways. The iconic rock group, the Rolling Stones, has screamed for years, "I Can't Get No Satisfaction." The song has become an anthem of the Rock and Roll generation. The old pop song, "Is That All There Is" suggests that we fill this void with pleasure. Yet those who have tried still come up empty.

Do you identify with this longing for more? If you do, then this book is for you. In it, you will discover the source of real life that

Introduction

everyone desires. You will see that the source of this life is a Person and not in things. You will discover that the whole purpose of Jesus coming to earth was to give us life and life more abundantly.

You will also see that receiving this life alone does not bring satisfaction. Many Christians have experienced new life but still struggle with a lack of fulfillment. You will discover that true happiness only comes when you allow this new life to manifest itself through you. This is the eternal purpose of God and why you were created.

So in the pages of this book, you will find the answer to these questions.

"What is the source of true happiness?"
"How can I overcome my selfishness and become a truly loving person?"
"How can I live up to all that I know?"
"How do I heal from the hurts of the past?"
"How can I get ahead in life and excel?"
"How can my life become truly significant?"
"If Christ lives in me why haven't I changed?"
"Why am I not experiencing the abundant life that Jesus promised?"

So let's get started and discover what real living is all about.

CHAPTER
One

There Is More Than One Kind of Life

That which is born of the flesh is flesh,
and that which is born of the Spirit is spirit.
Do not marvel that I said to you, 'You must be born again.

- Jesus, speaking to Nicodemus

Did you ever notice that Jesus said some crazy things? One day He asked a group of people to examine themselves to see if they had ears. He said if they had ears they would be able to hear him[1]. They must have looked at one another in bewilderment and thought, "We all have ears, what is he talking about?"

He told another gathering that He had come in order to give them life[2]. He said this to people who were alive, warm and breath-

---

1. Mark 4:9;
2. John 10:10;

ing. You can imagine the puzzled looks. He certainly knew how to get their attention. Even His disciples said these kinds of statements by Jesus were hard and difficult to understand.

> *Therefore, many of His disciples, when they heard this, said, "This is a hard saying; who can understand it?"*
>
> John 6:60

These sayings are hard to understand unless you grasp the one basic eternal truth that Jesus was trying to convey. There is more than one kind of life. He was talking to them about another kind of life – an inward life – a spiritual life that He would give them, which would manifest itself in abundance. Not necessarily an abundance of material things, but an abundance of the qualities of life that come from God's nature.

At creation, Man had a physical life and also a spiritual life.

Nicodemus expressed the same puzzlement when Jesus shared this exact truth with him. He had visited Jesus and inquired what he had to do to enter the Kingdom of God[3]. Jesus replied that he had to be born again. Nicodemus asked incredulously, "How can a man be born when he is old? Can he enter a second time into his mother's womb and be born?" Jesus went on to clearly explain to him that there were two kinds of life. There was a natural life and there was a spiritual life.

The natural life is outward and observable by our five senses.

---

3. John 3:1;

The spiritual life is inward and invisible to the natural senses. Even though the spiritual life is intangible, it does not make it any less real. The Bible tells us that the things that are seen are temporal but the things that are not seen are eternal.[4] You just need different senses to perceive them. In the latter case, they are spiritual senses. Thus we begin to understand Jesus' comments on "ears to hear" and "the blind leading the blind." [5]

Spiritual Life was first given to Man at Creation. He was created differently than animals. God formed the animals from the earth and they were complete. However, after God physically created Adam, He was not finished. He then proceeded to breathe into him the breath of life.[6] This was more than a physical breath of life; it was a spiritual breath of life. In that breath, God gave Adam a spiritual life that had the capability to connect with God's Life. At creation, Man had a physical life and also a spiritual life. His communion with God was both outward and inward.

Man Loses His Spiritual Life

It is important to see how Man lost his spiritual life. It is described in Genesis 3 where Adam and Eve ate the fruit of the Tree of the Knowledge of Good and Evil. This story can be viewed today as fanciful and incredulous, as did the sayings of Jesus long ago, but it portrays real spiritual truths that explain how man has come to his present condition today.

Here is how God described it: After creation, God put Man in a beautiful environment with a Tree of Life in the middle and each day was marked by God coming down and communing with Adam and

---

4. 2 Cor. 4:18;
5. Matt. 15:14;
6. Gen. 2:7;

Eve. The only condition for this to continue was that Man was not to eat of the fruit of the Tree of the Knowledge of Good and Evil. If he did, God said the day he ate of it, he would surely die. Satan entered the garden and tempted Adam and Eve by saying that they would not die if they ate of the fruit but rather, by eating it they would become like God deciding what was right and wrong. Adam and Eve partook of the fruit and immediately knew that they were naked. They were forced from the garden and their communion with God was cut off.

What do we learn from this? God put Man in an environment where his spiritual life was sustained by God's Life (The Tree of Life). He was unaware of right and wrong (naked but not ashamed). Man was warned that his spiritual life was contingent upon his continued innocence. He was not to claim (eat) for himself the right (fruit) to choose between good and evil (tree). God said that choice would kill him.

Man is not designed to determine for himself what is right and wrong. We are not to be our own boss but we are to humbly defer to God's lordship over our life. Satan's temptation was "If you eat of this fruit you will not die but you will be as God." [7] This is always Satan's temptation – be your own boss, there is no consequence. At first, it seemed that Satan was right. They ate the fruit, the day ended and they had not died. However, as we have seen, they possessed more than one kind of life, they also possessed a spiritual life. They had not died physically that day but they did die spiritually.

By ignoring God and deciding to run their own lives they had forced God to withdraw. They lost their communion with Him and were forced to go out and live their physical life without their spiritual life. The real tragedy for us is that they could only pass on their

---

7. Gen. 3:4;

physical life to their offspring. The consequence for us today is that every person that is a descendant of Adam has physical life only; we are missing out on spiritual life. Thus the Bible declares,

> ... through one man sin entered the world, and death through sin, and thus death spread to all men ...
> Romans 5:12

Paul writing to the Ephesians describes it as,

> ... dead in trespasses and sins.
> Ephesians 2:1

This is the state of every person that has been born into the world ever since. We have natural life but we are missing the Spiritual life that is meant to drive and energize it. We think that we have life but in reality, we have only the husk of life and the real kernel is missing. This is how Jesus saw the people of His day and why He declared to them that He had come that they may have life and life more abundantly.

Man is not designed to determine for himself what is right and wrong.

A Black and White World

Because of our spiritual void we all have a feeling that there must be something more to life. It is a universal longing. People try to fill this void with many things – pleasure, possessions, achievement

– but it is a God-shaped hole. The Bible declares that God has put eternity in our hearts.[8] Nothing of this earth can fill this vast spiritual emptiness. Only God can satisfy the longing of our soul because it is for Him and His Life that our soul was created.

> *Only God can satisfy the longing of our soul because it is for Him and His Life that our soul was created.*

Without His Life within, our existence can seem dull and bland. It can be likened to the difference between living in a black and white world or one in living colour. This is an area to which I have some experience as I am colour blind, particularly a red-green colour deficiency. The result, in my case, is that I have never seen certain colours. I have never seen green or purple or other secondary colours. I see these colours as other colours.

I first became aware of my deficiency in Grade One. My class was given a picture to colour and I excitedly reached into my crayon box and started to colour the grass in the picture. I remember my teacher, Mrs. Baines, coming down the aisle and looking at my sheet. She stopped and abruptly put her finger on my grass and sternly asked, "Why are you colouring your grass red."

It was quite traumatic and I didn't know what to say. I had simply taken the crayon out of the box that I thought matched the colour of grass. Yes, it is a strange world I live in. I do see beautifully manicured lawns as red. The point is, even though I was missing so

---

8. Eccl. 3:11;

Chapter One: *There Is More Than One Kind of Life*

much, I didn't realize it because to me my world was normal. It took someone who saw colours to reveal them to me.

As time went on, I became more and more conscious of the world that I was missing. As a child, I went with my parents on a Fall Sightseeing Tour to view the changing colours of the leaves. I remember sitting on the bus and gazing out on the forested landscape trying to understand why everyone was oohing and aahing. I have similar memories concerning rainbows and sunsets. I would wonder to myself, "What's the big deal." I was missing so much but I didn't realize it.

Our experience of salvation must include exercising our faith to receive the Holy Spirit.

Interestingly, it was only recently in life that it suddenly dawned on me why people liked to watch fireworks – it was the colours! How did I not realize that? I don't know why, but somehow, I thought that it was just the burst of different patterns that people admired. Again, I was unaware of what I was missing, I had become accustomed to the world I saw as normal.

Now, what if someone was totally colour blind – seeing only black and white – how would you describe what a world of colour was like? You could try to describe it but really they would have no idea how great the difference was. This only begins to describe the difference between having only a natural life, compared with having a spiritual life filled with Christ's Life.

> *We must turn from our independence from God and submit to His Lordship.*

Is it possible that many professing Christians have missed the colourful dynamic of Christ's life? They have grown up believing truths about Jesus' birth, teachings, death, and resurrection but have never received the power of His new Life within. Paul seemed to be concerned about this when he asked believers that he had met at Ephesus, "Did you receive the Holy Spirit when you believed?"[9] They responded that they had not even heard about the Holy Spirit. He proceeded to explain salvation to them and then lead them into the experience of receiving the Holy Spirit. Our experience of salvation must include exercising our faith to receive the Holy Spirit. All aspects of Christ life are received by faith. Every believer in Christ needs to believe by faith and experience the inward indwelling of His Life.

Jesus certainly knew the importance of this. Just before His ascension into Heaven, Jesus told His disciples to wait in Jerusalem for the outpouring of the Holy Spirit.[10] Paul writes to the Romans and explains that the Spirit they received was Christ in them who would give life to their natural bodies.[11] Even though Jesus Himself had taught the disciples the things pertaining to His Kingdom and commissioned them to go into all the world, He told them not to go yet, but to wait for the power that they would receive through His Spirit.[12]

---

9. Acts 19:2;
10. Acts 1:4;
11. Rom. 10:10-11;
12. Acts 1:8;

CHAPTER ONE: *There Is More Than One Kind of Life*

Are you Connected to the Power Source?

The power given to the followers of Jesus through the infilling of His Life was essential to their being able to fulfill their purpose. A good way to illustrate this is how an electric light bulb functions. An electric light bulb can only fulfill its purpose when it is connected to a power supply. In fact, it was designed and created for this. We cannot image a light bulb trying to produce light on its own. It could try by painting itself yellow but it would only be a cartoon image of its real potential.

So it is with us. We were created to shine and fulfill our destiny by the power of Christ's Life within. It is meant to be the central dynamo energizing and driving our life. It is the motor that empowers us to both achieve and accomplish our purpose. Without it, we are like a car with no motor. We may be able to move somewhat on the twelve-volt battery of our natural life but how incredibly short in comparison is that to a powerful 440 horsepower engine propelling us forward.

In the time of Jesus, the people knew nothing of cars and engines but they did know the power of water. Thus Jesus spoke to them and said,

> *If anyone thirsts, let him come to Me and drink. He who believes in Me, as the Scripture has said, out of his heart will flow rivers of living water. But this He spoke concerning the Spirit, whom those believing in Him would receive; for the Holy Spirit was not yet given, because Jesus was not yet glorified.*
>
> John 7:37-39

---

13. Matt.1:21;

Like the power of the water flowing over Niagara Falls that generates enough electricity for all of Southern Ontario, so is the power of the Holy Spirit flowing through our lives.

Jesus spoke this description in anticipation of the Holy Spirit's outpouring that would only be available after Jesus completed His work on earth and ascended to Heaven. You see, Jesus had to deal with the transgression of Man that had cut off God's Life in the beginning. The Scriptures tell us that the mission of Jesus was to save His people from their sins[13] and to lay down His Life as a ransom.[14]

When Jesus died on the cross He took the penalty for our sin and created a way for man to be welcomed back into that place of communion with God that Adam and Eve had forfeited in the beginning. Through faith in Christ, we can be forgiven and our hearts cleansed to be filled with God's Life again. It only takes a soft heart that repents of the first sin of Adam and Eve in the Garden.

We must turn from our independence from God and submit to His Lordship. We stop running our own lives and being our own boss. We humble ourselves and invite Christ into our heart. God is after our heart. His voice is still calling, "my son, my daughter, give me your heart."[15] Jesus said,

> He who loves his life will lose it, and he who hates his life in this world will keep it for eternal life.
>
> *Jn.12:25*

---

14. Mark 10:45;
15. Prov. 23:26

CHAPTER ONE: *There Is More Than One Kind of Life*

This was one of Jesus' hard sayings for those who first heard it. But I hope by now you know exactly what Jesus was saying. You have more than one life. If you try to keep your natural life to yourself, you will lose it; but if you yield your life to God you will receive His spiritual life. Why don't you take a moment right now and talk to the Lord? Surrender your life to Him. Ask to be filled with His Life. You can be spiritually born again!

CHAPTER
Two

The Facets of God's Life In You

> Be uniquely you. Stand out. Shine. Be colorful.
> The world needs your prismatic soul!
>
> *- Amy Leigh Mercree*

Now that you have received your new Life in Christ, what changes should you expect?

The moment you are born again a process begins which transforms you into the image of Christ. This image is not physical but spiritual. So, physically, you will not look much different than before except perhaps for a bit of a glow about you. They say that the eyes are the window to the soul, so, no doubt there will be a new sparkle about them.

The real change though begins on the inside. Your new life, energized by the Holy Spirit, begins to manifest itself in urges, promptings, and leadings. Much like a woman who becomes pregnant, you begin to feel the movement of the new life inside. When you are first saved, it is like a little baby Jesus is born in the cradle of your spirit. Like a baby, He is alive and present but doesn't exercise much control over His environment. At this stage, you are truly born again but you may still have a lot of your old attitudes, feelings and habits.

The Bible tells us that the process of change is complete when Christ comes to full stature within us.[16] The new Life in our spirit grows, moving out and possessing more and more areas of our mind, will and emotions and eventually expresses itself through our actions as we yield to its advance. Through the process, we die to our old life and are led by our new Life. This is spiritual growth.

This is not turning over a new leaf and trying to live by the teachings of Jesus. No, this is having Christ within, manifesting His Life through us.

Christ coming to full stature within us describes the state of His life completely filling us. His mind pushes out and fills our mind, His tongue fills our tongue, His hands push down our hands right to the fingertips. As a result, we think His thoughts, speak His words and do His bidding. We take on and express the character and attributes of Christ. These qualities of our new Life are listed in the Bible as love, joy, peace, longsuffering, kindness, goodness, faithfulness, gentleness, and self-control.[17] This is the fruit or product of the Spirit of Christ within.

---

16. Eph. 4:13;
17. Gal. 5:22-23;

It is important to note that this is *not* an exercise in self-effort. Remember what we said about the electric light bulb needing an energy force in order to shine. This is not turning over a new leaf and trying to live by the teachings of Jesus. No, this is having Christ within, manifesting His Life through us. Jesus referred to it as "abiding in the vine."[18] A branch does not produce fruit on its own. The fruit only grows as the branch maintains its connection with the vine – the source of Life.

The Garden of Our Heart

Let's look for a minute at how we grow spiritually. It is important that we understand the process and the part that we play and the part that we do not play. As we have seen, we can never generate God's Life on our own, that is the work of the Holy Spirit. However, we can influence the growth of His Life within. Jesus illustrated this in a parable He gave of a sower who sowed seed on different kinds of soil.[19] He explained that the condition of the soil determined the growth and yield of the crop. Let's follow His analogy for a moment. Jesus explained that the soils were representative of our hearts. Thus, it is the condition of our heart which determines how much the seed of life will grow and produce. Proverbs tells us to keep our heart with all diligence for out of it spring the issues of life.[20] We are to keep our hearts as we would keep the soil in a garden. A good gardener prepares the soil for planting, waters the plants and hoes the weeds. Plants grow better in soil that is cultivated, watered and free from weeds. Again, remember the gardener's work does not create the growth but it

---

18. John 15:4;
19. Matt. 13:3-23;
20. Prov. 4:23;

allows the growth to occur unhindered. We can never create the Life of Christ within but we are responsible for tending the soil of our heart where His Life grows. It is interesting to note that in the Garden of Eden before Man sinned, he was given the responsibility to tend the garden where the Tree of Life grew.

> *We can never create the Life of Christ within but we are responsible for tending the soil of our heart where His Life grows.*

The Prism of our Life

Many years ago I was teaching on the book of Ephesians and explaining Chapter 3:10-11.

The portion says,

> *So that through the church the manifold wisdom of God might now be made known to the rulers and authorities in the heavenly places. This was according to the eternal purpose that he has realized in Christ Jesus our Lord.*
>
> *Eph.3:10-11 (ESV)*

In the study, I was sharing that God's eternal purpose was to reveal Himself through the Church to the whole world. In His wisdom, God chose to show all the multi-faceted aspects of His Life and nature to the world through us, His church. After the service, a Romanian man came up to me and shared that in his Bible translation this verse stated that God would show forth His multi-colours through the Church. I later discovered that the Greek word, polupoikilos, translated as 'manifold', can just as accurately be translated 'many-coloured'.

Well, as I have shared, I am partially colour-blind and this description got my attention and started me thinking. God wants to reveal His colours to a black and white world through the church. My mind immediately went back to an experiment that we conducted in physics class in high school. You may remember it. A white light is shone through a triangular glass prism and projected on a screen. The angle of the prism diffracts the light and causes it to be projected on the screen in its colour spectrum of red, orange, yellow, green, blue, and violet. I thought how well this explains the verses in Ephesians. God is the white light that no man can see – but in order to reveal Himself, He has projected Himself through the prism of the Church so that the screen of the world could see Him in all His aspects. The prism is made up of you and me and every other Christian. We cannot produce the light on our own but we are the means God uses to reveal His colours to the world. He is using the different angles of our lives – our personalities, talents, circumstances, relationships, strengths and even weaknesses to show forth His glory to the world. This is why He created us in the first place, this was His eternal purpose.

Even though Paul knew nothing about this powerful analogy he came close to describing it in writing to the Corinthian church centuries ago.

But we all, with open face beholding as in a glass the glory of the Lord, are changed into the same image from glory to glory, even as by the Spirit of the Lord.
2 Corinthians 3:18

This verse shares that not only do we show forth Christ's glory but we do it in an ever increasing way. His image shines clearer and clearer through us. We are encouraged in Scripture to shine as bright lights in the world.[21] Notice that even though we cannot generate the light, we do have a responsibility in the process of shining. Jesus said to not hide our light under a bushel.[22] This tells us that it is possible to restrict the light. We can see in the prism analogy that the more transparent the glass, the more fully the light shines through. God is in the process of making us more and more transparent. This is another aspect of spiritual growth.

The Light of Life

So we see that we have a part to play in allowing Christ's light to shine through us. The source of the light is His Life. The scripture says of Jesus,

> *In him was life and the life was the light of men.*
> *John 1:4*

So it is with us, His Life within generates the light, and the more transparent we become, the more His multi-coloured nature and attributes are seen by others through us.

In researching this analogy of colours, I discovered that our eyes are colour-sensitive to only a small portion of the light spectrum. Because of this limitation, there are many colours that our eyes have never seen. Some have conjectured that part of the grandeur of Heaven may be the ability to see a whole new range of col-

---

21. Phil. 2:15;
22. Matt. 5:14-16;

CHAPTER TWO: *The Facets of God's Life In You*

ours. I hope it is so, it makes me feel a little better about my own colour blindness. I am limited to seeing only the three primary colours of red, blue and yellow, but someday I will see them all.

> *God is in the process of making us more and more transparent. This is another aspect of spiritual growth.*

Making it Simple

It is interesting to note that all the colours we see come out of the three primary colours. An artist knows that by mixing these three colours on his palette he can produce all the colours. There is a spiritual analogy to this. The spiritual life can seem so complicated and overwhelming that we do not know where to begin. How do I cooperate with God when I don't know where to start? Is it possible that God's light has some basic primary colours such that when you understand them you can produce the full spectrum of His character? If so, what are the primary aspects of Christ Life? What are the basic elements?

The Basic Facets of Life

Years ago I was praying and meditating on this very subject. I had just finished reading a business book that had studied companies that were at the top of their field and successful over an extended period of time.[23] The book claimed that they all had one thing in common, they all had narrowed their focus to the basic fundamentals of business. He described these three fundamentals as being:

---

23. In Search of Excellence

quality of product, service to customers and value in price. The companies who were successful all had at their core an excessive commitment to quality, service and value. All other aspects of their business came out of these basics.

> *The new Life that God has given us can be understood by gaining a better understanding of Love, Integrity, Forgiveness and Excellence or L.I.F.E.*

As I prayed, I told the Lord that I didn't want natural success in business but I wanted to be successful and excel in His Kingdom. I wanted to show forth His Life. I asked Him to show me the basic fundamentals of the Christian Life. I immediately thought of L, I, F, E and just as quickly the words Love, Integrity, Forgiveness and Excellence came to me.

I had no idea at the time how important and valuable this insight would be. Because as of now, it has become my basic understanding of the Life of Christ. Christ's Life is so large and all-encompassing, yet these four words have given me a handle on which I can lay hold of eternal Life. It is as if the light of Christ's Life can be shone through a prism and broken into Love, Integrity, Forgiveness and Excellence. I have discovered over time that these four aspects balance one another and can be mixed like the natural primary colours to produce all the beautiful shades and hues of the Christian Life. The practical implication to us is that the new Life that God has given us can be understood by gaining a better understanding of Love, Integrity, Forgiveness and Excellence or L.I.F.E. It is through these four aspects the Life of Christ will be manifest through us.

CHAPTER
Three

Making God Visible

To love another person is to see the face of God.

– *Victor Hugo (Les Miserables)*

If we are to express the image of God, it is natural to ask, "What does God look like? Well, here is where we have a problem. God is invisible.

The Bible teaches that God is spirit and undetectable to our physical, natural eyes. In fact, it was that way for much of human history. Before Jesus Christ came to earth, God had no living manifestation in the physical, natural world to which people could relate. He was only revealed through creation and the written Word. Then Jesus was born and walked the earth and the scriptures declared Him to be the image of God.

> *who being the brightness of His glory and the express image of His person...*
>
> *Hebrews 1:3*

Jesus was God manifest in the flesh – the physical expression of God. If you wanted to know what God was like, all you had to do was look at Jesus. If you wanted to see God's Love it was shown in Jesus' compassion for children and the hurt and wounded on earth. If you wanted to get a sense of God's judgment, you could find it in His words of condemnation to the hypocritical and insincere religious leaders of the day. The Life of Jesus was remarkable. It amazed and delighted, as well as dismayed and angered. His Life was a light that revealed the hearts of men. To this day, His life and teachings are revered and universally admired regardless of religious persuasion or lack thereof.

Just before Jesus left this earth and ascended into Heaven, He prayed that the glory that the Father had given Him would be given to His followers.[24] He then told His disciples that the Holy Spirit would be given to them and that He would guide and direct them and show them how to live.[25] The job of expressing God to the world passed from the physical body of Jesus to the Church. So as you may expect, the Church is called the Body of Christ.

> *... and gave Him to be head over all things to the church, which is His body, the fullness of Him who fills all in all.*
>
> *Eph. 1:22-23*

A story is told about a little boy in Sunday school. The teacher had given the children some free time to draw a picture. After a while, the

---

24. John 17:22;
25. John 16:13;

CHAPTER THREE: *Making God Visible*

teacher looked over the shoulder of a little boy, admiring his work. The child was drawing a picture of an old man with long hair and a beard. She asked him just who it was he was drawing. The boy answered, "I'm drawing a picture of God." The teacher responded, "God is a Spirit, no one has ever seen Him. No one knows what God looks like." The boy just smiled and said, "They will when I'm finished!"

What does God look like? Like the little boy, we are the answer to that question. God has determined that He will reveal Himself to the world through us. Those around us will know what God looks like by looking at our lives. Christ desires to dwell in us and express Himself through us. This is accomplished by the presence of the Holy Spirit within, regenerating our hearts. The Holy Spirit does His work by giving us new desires and prompting us to act like Christ. As we respond to these inner leadings we begin to express the Life of Jesus. This is the essence of Christian living. This is the abundant Life that Jesus promised.[26]

Those around us will know what God looks like by looking at our lives.

The Colours of Christ's Life

So what do people see when they look at your life? Do they see the pale expression of natural existence or do they see the radiant colours of a new Life in Christ shining through you?

We have seen that God is like white light. White light is brilliant and contains all the colours but they are not observable to the

---

26. John 10:10

human eye. It takes the material of a glass prism to draw out and display the "many coloured" aspects of His Life. As I shared in the previous chapter, I believe that there are four primary colours of Life that lift us out of a black and white world. These four aspects are Love, Integrity, Forgiveness and Excellence. These four aspects produce all the different hues and tints of God's L.I.F.E. that are to be seen through us.

You and I are the prisms that God uses. We are each unique in our own way. We have different personalities, talents and abilities. We live in different situations and circumstances. So, each of us will express His Life in ways that no one else can. This should excite and energize us.

You are significant – no one else can take your place. You matter to God. You were created for a purpose. As Paul wrote to the Galatians,

> *But when it pleased God, who separated me from my mother's womb and called me through His grace, to reveal His Son in me ...*
>
> *Gal. 1:15-16*

The difficulties that you face have a bigger purpose. If you respond to the leading of the Spirit through these times, unique tints and hues of His Life will be manifested through you.

Each of us will express His Life in ways that no one else can. This should excite and energize us.

CHAPTER THREE: *Making God Visible*

The Four Basic Colours

We have seen that the four basic aspects of Christ's L.I.F.E. are Love, Integrity, Forgiveness and Excellence. We should note that each of these divine aspects have a natural counterpart that is the result of trying to produce them on our own. But our efforts alone will only produce a faint black and white caricature of each that falls far short of their rich colour and texture.

I have found that as I have grown in my understanding of these four facets that it has helped me to better respond to the leadings of the Holy Spirit to express them. In the chapters to follow, I will describe each one more fully but for now, let me give a definition for each that attempts to show their true depth.

- Godly Love is giving unselfishly to the needs of others without regard to personal recognition or reward.

- Godly Integrity is living up to all that you know, or when failing to do so, freely confessing to God and others where you fall short.

- Godly Forgiveness is forgiving everybody all the time for everything before they ask or before they change.

- Godly Excellence is doing everything to the very best of your ability, as unto the Lord.

God wants to shine each of these four facets of His Life to the people around us. He deeply desires your neighbours, relatives, co-workers to see His love manifested through you. He wants you to walk in integrity so they encounter the honesty and righteousness of God. God wants you to show forgiveness so that they will know that He is forgiving. He also wants you to live your life in excellence so the individuals in your life will see the glory of God in everything you do.

We Have a Critical Role in Shining Forth God's L.I.F.E.

God's love, integrity, forgiveness, and excellence are not natural. They are far more than what we could generate in our human nature. They are the result of God's Life within, but their expression requires our cooperation. The Scripture clearly commands us to love, to live with integrity, to forgive, and to embrace excellence. God's Life is generated by the Holy Spirit within, but we have a critical role to play in releasing it. We must cooperate with the Spirit's transforming work in our hearts, and be diligent in expressing it.

Paul touches on this delicate balance and writes,

> *To this end I labour, striving according to His working which works in me mightily.*
>
> Col. 1:29

Here, Paul reveals that God places power and energy within us, and as we consciously choose to cooperate with God's plan, that power is released. A favourite illustration of mine demonstrates this dynamic well.

Imagine you are in your vehicle, out for a drive. As you come over a hill, you can see the road quickly comes to an abrupt stop at a T-intersection with a stone wall facing you on the other side. You need to stop – and fast. You have several options:

CHAPTER THREE: *Making God Visible*

- You could work to produce the desired result by your own power alone. In this scenario, you would open the door and drag your foot to try and slow the car down. This would be completely ineffective and only do damage to your shoe and foot.

OR

- You could see that your efforts would be insufficient and that the car was designed with power brakes, so you decide to trust the braking system to stop you. In this scenario, you would sit back and rest and do nothing. Unfortunately, although your trust is well placed, it would still end in disaster.

OR

- You could take action to engage the power brakes built into the vehicle. This would involve pressing down on the brake pedal. Your exerted effort would release the power of the braking system to stop the car.

Do not listen to the drum beat of religion which says, "Try harder." If you rely on your own efforts, you will either become frustrated or self-righteous.

We can understand this truth so clearly in the example above but I am amazed how many times in our spiritual lives we miss it. Many

Christians attempt to live the Christian life in their own strength only to become frustrated and discouraged. Others have a view that they should put forth no effort, and as a result, they grow lax and indifferent. We must understand that manifesting God's Life is not a work of the Holy Spirit alone; if that is your expectation, you will become too passive. It does require your commitment and effort.

However, it is not a result of your work alone either. Do not listen to the drum beat of religion which says, "Try harder." If you rely on your own efforts, you will either become frustrated or self-righteous. Neither is what God desires. It is not "either/or," it is "both/and." As a Christian, you are filled with Christ's Life and He will prompt you to act in a certain way. As you respond and put forth an effort, you release His power to take over and accomplish His work. The result is the release of His dynamic abundant Life.

With this background in mind let's go on and look at the first expression of God's L.I.F.E – Love.

CHAPTER *Four*

Love - The Impossible Commandment

*We know that we have passed from death to life,
because we love...
He who does not love... abides in death.*

- 1 John 3:14

Just What is Love?

We use the word love a lot, everywhere in fact. We love pizza. We love movies. We love our dogs. We love our cats. We love our parents. We love our spouse. We love our children. We love God.

Amazingly, we use the same word 'love' to describe how we feel about God – and pizza! Obviously, there is a big difference between God and pizza, and there is an equally significant difference between what 'love' means in these two contexts.

In the oldest manuscripts of Scripture, there are several different Greek words translated as 'love' in English. For example, "eros" is a love which is highly physical and sexual. Then there is "phileo", which is the type of love between brothers. There is also "agape", which portrays the kind of love that God has for man.

Our simple English word 'love' fails to capture the full range of complexity and emotion conveyed in these more specific Greek words. Since our vocabulary does such a poor job of communicating the meaning of love, is it any wonder that our culture's basic understanding of the nature of love is so muddled?

> *Man has discovered the meaning of "eros" love and "phileo" love but has not done too well in understanding and practicing "agape" love – God's love.*

We can learn from children who tend to see love from a fresh perspective. Their insights can be more instructive than those of many adults. The following responses were given by a group of 4 to 8-year-olds when asked: "what does 'love' mean?"

- "Love is when a girl puts on perfume and a boy puts on shaving cologne and they go out and smell each other."
- "Love is when you go out to eat and you give somebody most of your French fries without making them give you any of theirs."
- "Love is when someone hurts you and you get so mad, but you don't yell at them because you know it would hurt their feelings."
- "Love is when mommy makes a coffee for my daddy and she takes a sip before giving it to him to make sure the taste is okay."

CHAPTER FOUR: *Love – The Impossible Commandment*

- "When my grandma got arthritis, she couldn't bend over and paint her toenails anymore, so my grandfather does it for her all the time, even when his hands got arthritis too. That's love."
- "During my piano recital, I was on a stage and scared. I looked at all the people watching me and saw my daddy waving and smiling. He was the only one doing that. I wasn't scared anymore. That's love."
- "Love is when you tell a guy you like his shirt, then he wears it every day."
- "Love is like a little old woman and a little old man who are still friends even after they know each other so well."
- "My mommy loves me more than anybody. You don't see anyone else kissing me to sleep at night."
- "Love is when your puppy licks your face even when you left him alone all day."
- "Love is what's in the room with you at Christmas time if you stop opening presents and listen."
- "You really shouldn't say I love you unless you mean it, but if you mean it, you should say it a lot. People forget."

Their responses provide some deeply profound meanings, and hilariously observant ones as well. As interesting and funny as these definitions are, they also underscore the variety of interpretations and layers packed into our word 'love'. We are still faced with the question, "what is love?"

What is Godly Love?
Man has discovered the meaning of "eros" love and "phileo" love but has not done too well in understanding and practicing "agape"

love – God's love. To discover the true, eternal definition of God's love we must turn to the Bible. There are two verses that help us to understand the definition of God's love. Interestingly, they have corresponding references, John 3:16 and 1 John 3:16.

> *For God so loved the world that He gave His only begotten son, that whoever believes in Him should not perish, but have everlasting life.*
>
> *John 3:16*

> *By this we know love, because He laid down His life for us. And we also ought to lay down our lives for the brethren.*
>
> *I John 3:16*

The first verse tells us that God's love caused Jesus to lay down His life for us. The second verse tells us that we express God's love by similarly laying down our lives for others. There are three implications from these verses.

Love is giving – you cannot express love without some aspect of giving.

1. The Essence of God's Love is Giving

God so loved the world that He gave. In these two passages, John has identified the central core of love, as demonstrated by God Himself. God so loved the world that He gave His very life so that He could purchase salvation for every living being. The essence of love is giving. Victor Hugo, in his classic work Les Miserables, penned a line that sums this up so well:

> "You can give without loving, but you can't love without giving."

Love is giving – you cannot express love without some aspect of giving. But giving can be motivated by different things. Let's dig a little deeper.

2. The Focus of God's Love is Always on Others

Jesus gave His life motivated by meeting the needs of others. Salvation was our greatest need and He endured the cross for our benefit. His love caused Him to take our place and suffer the penalty for our sins. He gave Himself thinking of us. He endured the cross focused on the joy that He would have in our salvation.

> Looking unto Jesus ... who for the joy that was set before Him endured the cross, despising the shame ...
> Heb.12:2

God's love in Jesus caused Him to focus on our need rather than His own comfort and it resulted in our redemption. This is an integral understanding in formulating a definition of true, Godly love.

3. The Motive Behind God's Love is Unselfish

Love puts others first before ourselves, but it is not with a hidden agenda. Love does not give in order to manoeuvre or jockey for increased recognition or rewards in this life. Love is acting with the best interest of the other person at heart; it is choosing their best, ahead of your own. This was the love that Jesus acted upon. The scripture states,

> *For even Christ did not please Himself...*
> *Romans 15:3*

and

> *Let this mind be in you which was also in Christ Jesus, who, being in the form of God, did not consider it robbery to be equal with God, but made Himself of no reputation, taking the form of a bondservant, and coming in the likeness of men. And being found in appearance as a man, He humbled Himself and became obedient to the point of death, even the death of the cross.*
> *Philipians 2:5-8*

Summarizing,
- the essence of love is giving
- the focus of love is others
- the motive of love is unselfish

Love is acting with the best interest of the other person at heart; it is choosing their best, ahead of your own.

CHAPTER FOUR: *Love – The Impossible Commandment*

These three elements form our working definition of love:

God's Love gives unselfishly to the needs of others, without regard to personal recognition or reward.

This is the Love of God. John 3:16 tells us that we see this love as God gave His Son for us. 1 John 3:16 tells us that this love is what God wants to place in our hearts so we, in turn, can extend it to others. Extending God's Love is the first expression of Christ's L.I.F.E.

Extending love is mission critical and is the first distinguishing mark of the new Life God has given us. This love is fundamental to who we are called to be, and it is at the centre of how we are to act in our daily lives. This love is truly revolutionary and counter-cultural. This love changes hearts and minds. But without practical, tangible, observable action, this love will remain only words and a nice definition. The application of this love is impossible without the Life of Christ as its source.

Extending love is mission critical and is the first distinguishing mark of the new Life God has given us.

Without Christ's Life inside of us, the only love we will be capable of extending is natural human love. Human love revolves around itself; it is a shallow mirage, a pale imitation of the vibrant life-altering Love of Jesus.

Natural Love, At Its Core, Is All About 'Me'

Basically, human love is only a feeling. We 'love' someone because of the way that person makes us feel. "I love you", most times mean, "I love how you make me feel."

So when with human love we say, "I love you", we are actually saying,

- "I love how you love me."
- "I love what you do for me."
- "I love how you benefit me."
- "I love being around you."
- "I love the attention you give me."
- "I love how you make me feel important."
- "I love how you give me a sense of value."
- "I love how you lift up my self-esteem."
- "I love the feeling of pride and well-being that you give me."

And when we say, "I don't love you anymore", we are really saying,

- "I don't love how you make me feel."
- "I don't love being around you."
- "I don't love the attention you give me."

When we experience God's Love first, we can then respond with overflowing love to those around us.

CHAPTER FOUR: *Love – The Impossible Commandment*

Human love is responsive. Human love is self-centred. It primarily exists because of the good feelings another person or thing inspires in us.

Human Love Can Only Extend Love After It Has First Received It

Naturally, as humans, we love people who love us. It is very difficult to love people who are not loving. I remember hearing a preacher speaking about the necessity of loving one another. He elaborated on this point at some length before finally making this incredible statement, "Don't you just hate people who don't love?"

His statement reveals the problem we face: we know we should love people. We know we should love our enemy. We know we should love those who spitefully use us, but somehow we cannot bring ourselves to do it. As long as we are limited to natural, responsive love, we are restricted to only love those who love us.

If natural love is so at odds with God's love, how can we as human beings love with Godly love? Do not even begin to try or you will be frustrated and discouraged; it is impossible. We cannot do it on our own. We need the new Life in Christ we have been sharing about. Only then can we receive His Love and channel it to the people around us.

The key is to tap into the source of Love – God Himself. When we experience God's Love first, we can then respond with overflowing love to those around us. Godly Love is giving, and you cannot give Love unless you have received Love. God who designed us knows this and has poured out His Love in our hearts.

> *... the love of God has been poured out in our hearts by the Holy Spirit who was given to us.*
>
> Romans 5:5

When we experience His Love, we are then able to love others.

Notice The Command to Love

We are directly commanded to love. According to our definition, we are commanded to give unselfishly to the needs of others without regard to personal recognition or reward. The Apostle John makes it abundantly clear – showing God's Love is not optional.

> *...and this is His commandment that we should believe on the name of his son, Jesus Christ and love one another as he gave us commandment.*
>
> 1 John 3:23

When John references 'His commandment', he is pointing his readers back to the passage found in John 15:12, where Jesus himself gives the same pointed direction:

> *...and this is my commandment that you love one another as I have loved you.*
>
> Jn.15:12

Love Isn't Optional

Jesus commands us to love as "I have loved you," not as we would naturally love one another with human love. Marriage should be based on God's Love not human love.

CHAPTER FOUR: *Love – The Impossible Commandment*

A wedding ceremony, I witnessed years ago stands out in my mind. The couple did not want a church wedding and were married by a ship's captain. At first glance, it appeared fairly typical: a lovely bride, handsome groom, and friends and family beaming around them. What stood out to me, however, were the wedding vows.

The couple said that they would be "united as long as they both shall love." I thought to myself, this isn't going to last very long; this marriage could be over quite quickly. A marriage based on human love 'as long as we both shall love' has a flimsy foundation. As soon as either the new husband or wife acts unloving for a period of time, the other spouse no longer feels love and feels justified in ending the marriage.

Sad to say, the divorce rates reflect this. Current statistics indicate that close to half of all marriages break up – I suggest that is because, nearly half of the time, someone is not very loving. But there is a different possible outcome. They could decide to love each other with God's Love that does not depend on how it is treated.

God's Love gives unselfishly to the needs of others, without regard to personal recognition or reward.

If love is a feeling, then a command to love is pointless.

Love is a Decision, not a Feeling

Jesus commands us to love. This command itself reveals that our human understanding of love is faulty. If love is a feeling, then a command to love is pointless. How can I be commanded to feel a certain way? We think, "I either love or I don't love." But no, love is not just a feeling. It is a decision – a choice. God chose to extend love to us, regardless of how undeserving we were. Paul wrote about this in Romans,

> *God demonstrates His own love toward us, in that while we were still sinners, Christ died for us.*
> *Romans 5:8*

Christ laid down His life for us when we were miserable, sinful, and unloving. And this unbelievable selfless act of giving is the example Jesus commands us to emulate as well:

> *This is my commandment, that you love one another as I have loved you.*
> *John 15:12*

Producing Godly Love in your Life is Impossible - but Simpler than You Think

God has provided an avenue for us to extend His Love effortlessly. He isn't commanding us to work and sweat and cut against the grain of our human nature to do it. We don't have to convert and change our human feelings in order to obey Jesus' command.

Love is not just a feeling.
It is a decision – a choice.

No, we reach beyond ourselves and draw upon the Love that comes from our new Life in Christ. We reach into God's reservoir

CHAPTER FOUR: *Love – The Impossible Commandment*

of Love and allow it to flow through us. We can then express God's Love to those we come in contact with. Godly Love flows effortlessly into the lives of others, as we simply focus on God's Love for us! As we receive His Love into our lives, it fills us and overflows into the lives of others. As 1 John 4:19 states,

> *We love because He first loved us.*
> *1 John 4:19 (NU-text)*

On our own, it is impossible to show this kind of Love. We must be plugged into God, and allow the current of God's Love to run into and through us. Remember our illustration of the light bulb only being able to shine when connected to the electrical source. Connected to the power supply, the bulb will shine effortlessly and project light into every corner of the room. So with us, the effort we put forth is not to love but to maintain our connection with the source of Love.

> *So with us, the effort we put*
> *forth is not to love but to*
> *maintain our connection with*
> *the source of Love.*

To do that, we must understand what God's Love is in simple practical terms and what breaks our connection and restricts its flow through us.

The first step is to ask a simple question. Am I a Giver, or am I a Taker?

Givers or Takers

We are all born as Takers. We all come into this world, grasping, with a taker attitude. If you doubt that, think of newborn babies and it will become quite apparent. Small children are only concerned with their own needs. They don't care if it is 3:30 am. They don't care if you are exhausted. They don't care if you have something else going on. If they are hungry, or they want a toy, they will let you know. As we grow into adulthood, we learn to mask and temper our taker attitude, yet it remains under the surface, central to our being.

The distinguishing mark of Christians is their unusual remarkable Love.

God wants to transform us. He wants to change us from a Taker to a Giver. By being 'born again' and receiving His Spirit He begins this truly amazing, supernatural transformation from the inside out. He puts his Love in our hearts and as we draw upon it, we find it satisfies all our wants and desires, freeing us to become a giver to the needs of others.

Jesus said,

By this, all will know that you are My disciples, if you have love for one another.

John 13:35

The distinguishing mark of Christians is their unusual remarkable Love. Just as you or I leave fingerprints on everything that we

CHAPTER FOUR: *Love – The Impossible Commandment*

touch, so the fingerprints that are to be left by Christians in the lives of those they touch are acts of Love.

The Taker's Attitude vs The Giver's Attitude

A taker approaches every circumstance and situation with their own needs, goals, and lives in the forefront of their mind. They tend to ask questions like:

- "What's in it for me?"
- "How will this affect me?"
- "How will I benefit as a result of this?"
- "What will this cost me?"
- "How will I be inconvenienced?"
- "How will I profit from this?"
- "How will I get credit for this?"
- "How will I benefit from this?"

Whereas a giver's attitude is just the opposite. It cuts against every selfish bone in our body. In the circumstances and situations Givers find themselves, they ask questions like:

- "What's in this for others?"
- "How will this benefit the other individual?"
- "What will this cost them?"
- "What will be the inconvenience to the other individual?"
- "How can I give the credit to them?"
- "How can I give the profit to them?"

It is impossible to change ourselves from being a Taker to being a Giver. We cannot simply snap our fingers and change. However, we can look to Christ and say, "Lord, I want to be a Giver. I want my mind renewed. I want to think differently. I want to realize what it really means to be Christian. Fill me with Your love."

> *Being a Christian means being a Giver.*
> *How incredibly sad it is when*
> *we call ourselves Christians,*
> *while ignoring His call to Love.*

Christ is a Giver; He Laid Down His Life for Us.

Being a Christian means being a Giver. How incredibly sad it is to call ourselves Christians, while ignoring His call to Love – the single most defining attribute of Christ's Life. Jesus was a Giver and out of Love He laid down His life for us, and His clear intention for us is to follow His example.

Again hear the Apostle John's remarks,

> *Hereby we perceive the love of God because He laid down his life for us, and we ought to lay down our life for our brothers.*
> *1 John 3:16*

As John rightly points out, Jesus laid down His life for us, but it was not only when He literally gave His life on the cross as a substitute for us. No, He laid down His life from the very beginning of His ministry right to the end. He carried His cross His entire ministry. Jesus was always laying down His life for others.

Why do you think Jesus prayed at night or early in the morning? Was there some special benefit in praying when it was dark outside?

CHAPTER FOUR: *Love – The Impossible Commandment*

No. Jesus prayed at night because His waking daylight hours were given to other people, in love.

People constantly pressed in upon Him and Jesus never denied them; He received them willingly and gladly. His disciples would say 'Don't bother the Master' or 'Keep the children back', yet Jesus instructed, 'No, let the little children come to Me.' He was constantly ministering to the needs of other people. He was laying down His Life for others, every single day.

Why was Jesus able to sleep in a boat during a storm? It wasn't because he had some divine sleeping ability! No, I believe it was because He was absolutely exhausted. Jesus constantly gave His time and energy for other people – to the point that the moment He was alone in the boat, He fell asleep. He slept right through a raging storm.

> *Jesus laid down His life for others and we ought to lay down our lives for others.*

Are You a Giver?

Jesus laid down His life for others and we ought to lay down our lives for others. Are you a Christian? Are you showing Christ's Life? We might say we are Givers, but the proof is in the pudding. How do we act?

- When you get an extra hundred dollars, what goes through your mind? Do you dream of ways to spend it for your own benefit – or do you think of how you could help others with it?

- When there is a free hour in your schedule, do you think of ways to spend that hour for your own benefit – or for the benefit of others?
- When you look at your possessions, do you constantly think of ways to benefit yourself, or others?

Love is the primary identifier of the Christian Life. We are called to be Givers, and we need to have this expression in our lives if we are going to be Christians. There is no sense calling ourselves Christians without understanding, embracing, and demonstrating God's Love for one another. It is by love that we are to be known to the world; love is meant to be the hallmark of Christianity.

> *By this, all will know that you are My disciples, if you have love for one another."*
>
> John 13:35

Love Runs Much Deeper Than Words

The expression of love for many Christians is only tongue-deep. They speak words of love but their lives are shallow in the practical demonstration of it. When it really matters, when it comes down to the crunch, they act in their own interest. The love that they express is of the human variety and lacks depth and substance.

In contrast, God demonstrated that His Love is giving away the thing nearest and dearest even when it is not appreciated. Jesus stayed on the cross, laying down His life for the very people who stood at the crucifixion scene mocking and ridiculing Him. They taunted,

> *... If You are the Son of God, come down from the cross.*
>
> Mt. 27:39

CHAPTER FOUR: *Love – The Impossible Commandment*

> *The expression of love for many Christians is only tongue-deep. They speak words of love but their lives are shallow in the practical demonstration of it.*

Jesus easily could have come down from the cross and proven His identity. He could have said, "Well, I need to stand for truth here. I truly am the Son of God, so I will come down." But He didn't.

Jesus showed us what God's Love looks like. This same Love has been poured into our hearts by the Holy Spirit. We have the same capacity to share it with others – if we choose to follow the leading and prompting of God's Spirit within us. God's Love must be expressed through our tangible body. Just as white light is diffracted through a glass prism to show the colours of the rainbow, so God's Love diffracts through the circumstances of our lives to show the world what He is really like. He wants us to lay down our lives for others. This is the mark of being a Christian.

Right now, you have a decision to make. The Holy Spirit will lead you to show God's Love to others, but you must choose to cooperate. If not, you will stifle God's Life showing through you and grieve the Holy Spirit, and miss out on truly diffracting God's nature and likeness.

Who are You Living for?

I have heard the expression used when busy people are asked to assist someone else, "I would like to help but I only have two hands." They mean that they are limited and their hands are already full with other responsibilities. The only way they could help would be to lay something down in order to have a free hand. In the same way, you only have one life, you will either use it to benefit yourself or others, you cannot do both. This is why the scripture says that we ought to lay down our life for others. You only have one life. A decision has to be made as to what it will be all about? You will either live it for yourself, or you will live it for others.

> *You only have one life, you will either use it to benefit yourself or others, you cannot do both.*

Some time ago, I had a conversation with an auto mechanic. He told me a story that really made this concept come alive for me.

He said, "You know, it used to bother me that my friends were always asking me to help them to fix their car. I was finding that every Saturday, my day off, I was under the hood of another car. I began to feel used and resentful. Then, I read this verse about laying down our lives for others, and I felt the Holy Spirit ask me, 'Are you willing to lay down your Saturday for others?' Immediately I understood what laying down my life would mean to me. Was I willing? In that moment I made a decision. I would plan to work on a friend's car every weekend. From that time on, Saturdays became my greatest joy and pleasure.

I must add that saying 'yes' to God's internal prompting, or choosing to have a 'Giving attitude,' does not mean we never put boundaries around our lives. To not do so would hinder us from showing God's Love in the long run. We all need a certain degree of structure and balance in our schedules. Nonetheless, being a Giver is a shift in attitude that lays down our own preferences, prior-

CHAPTER FOUR: *Love – The Impossible Commandment*

ities, and desires – for the benefit of others. When we do this in the power of God's Love, we experience a joy and satisfaction that far exceeds any pleasure of self-indulgence.

We are Called to Demonstrate Love

Givers look at interruptions and impositions differently than others; 'being used' suddenly becomes an opportunity to show the Love of God. In Matthew 5:41, Jesus teaches that being compelled to go one mile is a platform to demonstrate God's love by volunteering to go the second mile.

Growing in love or expressing love requires a series of switches in perspective. Rather than looking to acquire something you highly value, Love will have you looking for ways to give that thing away. Time, money, possessions – whatever you give away that is precious to you, is a demonstration of true Love.

Time, money, possessions – whatever you give away that is precious to you, is a demonstration of true Love.

When I was a young man, I witnessed on a small scale an excellent demonstration of this sort of love on a trip to India. My role on the trip was as an assistant to two outstanding spiritual leaders, a missionary evangelist named Billy Cole, and a superintendent of missions named Harry Schism.

Harry had a smaller sized Bible, which was rare in those days. It was very convenient; he was able to keep it in his coat pocket and carry it with him wherever he went. He used it all the time and the margins were full of reflections he had written. One day, in my presence, Billy remarked to Harry, "My, that's a really nice Bible!" He leafed through it admiringly and said, "Boy, I wish I had a Bible like that. Where did you get it?" In response, Harry took the Bible from his hand, opened up the fly leaf, took his pen and wrote on it, "To my friend Billy Cole, from Harry Schism" then he gave the Bible back to Billy. I still remember Billy's response, "Oh no, don't do that! You need it and you have your notes in there." But Harry put the Bible back into Billy's hands and said, "I want you to have it. It's yours. Keep it and enjoy it."

This made a huge impression on me; I thought, "what an outstanding expression of love." I can just imagine how that would have made me feel if someone had done that for me. The Bible was a very personal gift; though it wasn't outrageously expensive, Harry Schism gave it from a free heart because he cared for the friendship he had with Billy Cole.

It is in the little things of life that God wants to show Himself – just as much as the big things. Most of us are not going to be asked to literally lay down our life for someone else, but God prompts us to show Love in the little things: the way we speak to our spouse, how we talk to our kids, our attitudes towards our family, work, and church. Each time it requires the laying down of a little part of our lives.

> *Most of us are not going to be asked to literally lay down our life for someone else, but God prompts us to show Love in the little things*

This prompting is constantly coming forth from inside of us, and we must choose to align our will with the purpose of God. Our response should be, "Yes Lord, I will recognize these opportunities that you give me to lay down my life to bless other people."

As Jesus promises, you will discover it is far more blessed to give than it is to receive.[27] These expressions of love will give us more joy or satisfaction than a life lived only serving our own wants and desires.

> *Our expression of love for others is the greatest example of God's power.*

The Power of Love

Paul writes to the church in Thessalonica, reminding them of how he and his team first shared the Gospel with them. He writes,

> *For our gospel did not come to you in word only but also in power and in the Holy Spirit and in much assurance...*
> 1 Thess. 1:5

When Paul writes that the gospel came to them with a demonstration of power, our minds tend to think that there must have been a dramatic display of 'signs and wonders'. Miracles definitely did happen in the ministry of Paul while he traveled to share the gospel, but is this what he meant here? As we read further in this verse it reveals that Paul was referring to something else:

---

27. Acts 20:35

> *... as you know what kind of men we were among you for your sake.*
>
> 1 Thess.1:5

According to this verse, the power of the Gospel was demonstrated in how Paul and his team conducted themselves – and Paul explains specifically how they acted in the next chapter.

> *For our exhortation did not come from error or uncleanness, nor was it in deceit but as we have been approved by God to be entrusted with the gospel, even so, we speak not as pleasing man but God who tests our hearts for neither at any time did we use flattering words nor cloak for covetousness God as witness. Nor did we seek glory from men, either from you or from others. When we might have made demands as apostles of Christ. But we were gentle among you, just as a nursing mother cherishes her own children affectionately longing for you. We were well pleased to impart to you not only the gospel of God but our own lives because you had become dear to us.*
>
> 1 Thessalonians 2:3-8

Paul and his friends shared the gospel, in the power of love. It was demonstrated in the gentle, unselfish and Godly way they cared and treated those they ministered to.

Do you realize that it takes more of God's power to open spiritual eyes than to open blind natural eyes? Do you know that walking uprightly in love requires more of God's power than causing a man to walk with lame legs? Jesus healed people by speaking words, hearing His voice, the blind and lame were made whole. What did it cost Jesus – only His breath.

CHAPTER FOUR: *Love – The Impossible Commandment*

But what was the cost to Him to heal our hearts? What was the cost to Him to change our sinful nature? What was the cost to Him to pour His Love in our hearts by the Holy Spirit? It cost Jesus His very life; He had to die in order to accomplish that. There was no other way.

Our expression of love for others is the greatest example of God's power. As Christians, we are called to speak the gospel to other people, the words we use are meant to be accompanied by power – the power of God's Love demonstrated through our actions. Jesus said,

> *By this, all will know that you are My disciples, if you have love for one another.*
>
> John 13:35

Is the mark of Love in your life? If someone examined your life for evidence proving you were a Christian, would they find it?

Obeying the Command to Love

Jesus says,

> *This is my commandment: that you love one another as I have loved you. Greater love has no one than this than to lay down one's life for his friends.*
>
> John 15:12-13

Jesus is not giving us an option. We are commanded to love – and as we determined earlier, love is not a feeling we wait for – it is a choice we make.

Obeying the command to love, however, does not mean we try really hard to love. As I have shared, a light cannot emit light without electrical power, so we cannot love as God commands us to on our own. If we try, we will fail. We will come short, and find ourselves frustrated. Obeying the command to love is like turning the light switch on. It starts with simply saying, 'Yes.'

Switching the analogy, think about the tap in your kitchen or bathroom. There may be water in the pipes supplied from the city reservoir and sufficient pressure to move the water but there will be no flow until you turn on the tap. Turning the tap does not manufacture the water or provide the pressure, but the act of turning the valve releases the power of the system to provide the water. Your part is turning on the tap, everything else happens without your effort.

Similarly, as believers, we are connected to the source of Love. We also have the pressure of the Holy Spirit who is constantly prompting and leading us with inner urges. Turning on the tap is simply choosing to follow the Holy Spirit's leading. Our choice to obey the command to love is necessary in order to experience the flow of God's Love through us. We cannot manufacture the Love or produce its power, that is the work of God, but we hold the choice to release it.

Love requires a new schedule.

Sadly, many Christians have never exercised this choice. They have never made the definitive step of deciding to cooperate with the Holy Spirit. God has put the source of His deep Love within them but the tap in their life is closed. Rather than having a mindset of love, they have defaulted to their self-first "Taker mentality."

So you get to choose – will you turn on the tap or not? Will you view an 'imposition' as a disruption to your schedule, timeline, or

CHAPTER FOUR: *Love – The Impossible Commandment*

budget – or will you see it as an opportunity to be exactly what you were called to be as a Christian? Opening the tap allows God's Love to spring forth, like a river of living water, into the lives of those around you.

Mental Obstacles

Saying 'yes' to God's command to love requires overcoming the mental roadblocks that hinder us from acting. Here are a few.

"I wish I had time to do something for others – but I just don't. You will have to find somebody who has more time than I do."

But is this statement true? Have some been given more time than others? Of course not, we all have the same amount of time. What the person should have said is, "I have already filled my time for me – with what I want to do."

Love requires a new schedule. We have all been given 24 hours to spend each day. We can choose to use our schedule for our own self-interest, or for the interests of others. Obeying the commandment to love means laying aside chunks of time to invest in others, pouring God's Love into them. Don't fill your 24 hours totally with self-interest. Leave time for the interests of others.

Here is another one.

"I'd like to help others out financially, but I just don't have the money."

When we choose to obey Jesus' command to love, we open the windows of Heaven over our lives and He pours out more blessings than we are able to receive.

Many times resources are lacking because we have used every nickel and dime that comes our way for ourselves, and have even borrowed additional money to get what we want. As a result, we have limited ourselves in obeying the leading of the Spirit to help others. Love requires setting a different kind of budget – a budget that designates a certain percentage to be given to others. If we feel there is not enough money for this, remember, God is our source of income, not our job. God is well able to give us funds from unexpected sources. Jesus taught this truth in Luke,

Give, and it will be given to you: good measure, pressed down, shaken together, and running over will be put into your bosom. For with the same measure that you use, it will be measured back to you.

Luke 6:38

When we choose to obey Jesus' command to love, we open the windows of Heaven over our lives and He pours out more blessings than we are able to receive.

Having the Face of Jesus

When I was just a young minister, I met an elderly gentleman while attending a conference. During our conversation, he shared his story with me.

In the height of the 1920's, this man played the stock market heavily, enjoying an ever increasing lifestyle as the market skyrocketed. Then, the great market crash of 1929 happened – and he lost everything. I can still remember his words.

"When I realized that I had nothing – all my money was gone, my stocks were worthless, and everything had been taken from me

Chapter Four: *Love – The Impossible Commandment*

– I stood out on a balcony high above the city one night thinking about jumping. I looked out over the cityscape and I saw a cross not far away, all lit up in the night. Something deep inside of me said, 'go there'. Rather than jumping, I went down and walked towards it. The lit cross was over a harbour mission, a place where homeless men could get food and shelter. I went in, got in the lineup and I received my supper. All of us sat through a bit of a talk and then were given blankets. We all bedded down in this big room to sleep. I lay there feeling so empty, so lost, and asking God if He could just help me in some way. Then, I felt a hand on my shoulder. I turned over, and I looked up; a man stood over me and said, 'Come with me, I'm taking you home'. He took me to his house, fed me, clothed me, gave me a room to stay in, and helped me get back up on my feet. This man turned out to be a Christian, and he led me to Jesus, and is the reason I'm in the ministry today." He finished by telling me, "When he touched my shoulder and I looked up I saw Jesus in the face of a man."

I have never forgotten that last sentence – even after all these years. That is exactly what God wants to do. He wants to show His face in our face. He wants our hands to be His hands. He wants our voice to be His voice. God wants to make His Life and His character visible through our life. This is the whole goal of being a Christian, showing the Love of God very practically, very tangibly, through our life.

Many years ago, I read an article in Reader's Digest written by Hilary Lorman. Let me share the essence of it with you as it illustrates so well what God desires to do through our lives.

A psychiatric nurse stationed in Kansas City was given a referral to visit an elderly woman, Mrs. Cameron. Hilary, the nurse, made her way to the decaying apartment building where her new patient lived.

Many of Hilary's patients fought heartbreaking battles against chronic mental illness, and some were left helpless by their struggles. She counted on her faith in God to carry her through the rough cases she had to deal with. After much knocking, Mrs. Cameron hesitantly and fearfully opened the door. A faded housecoat covered her gaunt body and she was wearing an oversized pair of men's shoes. The sunless apartment had a stale smell of bacon and the sink was filled with greasy dishes. The referral notice listed no family or emergency contact and stated that she had resisted all attempts to get her into a nursing home.

> *God wants to make His Life and His character visible through our life. This is the whole goal of being a Christian, showing the Love of God very practically, very tangibly, through our life.*

A wild look of suspicion crossed Mrs. Cameron's face when Hilary asked her again to consider a nursing home. Feeling a sense of futility, Hilary asked if she was hungry. When she nodded yes, the young nurse went into the kitchen and opened the refrigerator. There she saw a half container of sour milk, stale bread, one egg and a package of sausages. Turning to the table she saw a yellowed copy of the Lord's prayer hanging on the wall. She thought to herself, Lord, I don't understand you. How could you forget her, how could you forget this poor old lady.

Hilary washed up the dishes and while water heated in the enamel kettle, she browned the sausages, made toast, and scram-

CHAPTER FOUR: *Love – The Impossible Commandment*

bled the egg. Taking the food to Mrs. Cameron, she saw the elderly woman's face soften and then nod yes when she said she was going to take her to see the doctor. Hilary phoned and arranged for her admission to the hospital and then called for a cab. As she settled her into the back seat, Mrs. Cameron squeezed her hand and said, "Thank you… thank you … you are an answer to prayer." In that moment a feeling of awe swept over Hilary and she sensed the voice of God say to her, "I have not forgotten her, I sent you".

CHAPTER
Five

Integrity - Honesty with God and Others

Integrity is doing the right thing, even when no-one is watching.
- C. S. Lewis

We have now seen how incredibly significant love is. It is the first aspect of the Life that God has given us. Now let's consider the next component of L.I.F.E. – Integrity.

There is a natural progression from Love to Integrity. The Apostle John in his epistle reveals that there is no practical showing of Love without Integrity.

> "But whoever has this world's goods, and sees his brother in need, and shuts up his heart from him, how does the love of God abide in him?" My little children, let us not love in word or in tongue, but in deed and in truth. And by this, we know that we are of the truth, and shall assure

our hearts before Him. For if our heart condemns us, God is greater than our heart and knows all things. Beloved, if our heart does not condemn us, we have confidence toward God.

1 John 3:17-21

John is saying that we should not just be talking about our love, we need to practically express it. If we do not follow through on what we say, our hearts will condemn us. Simply put, John is speaking about integrity. He instructs that the only way for our hearts to have confidence before God is to live out what we believe. Integrity is living out all that we say and believe. God has integrity – He is just who He is – and if we are to have His Life expressed through us, we need to live in integrity.

Love comes out of a pure heart, a good conscience, and sincere faith. Pure, good, sincere: each of these adjectives reflects a different facet of integrity.

Paul's letter to Timothy demonstrates that Godly love grows out of integrity. Integrity is the seed plot.

Now the purpose of the commandment is love from a pure heart, from a good conscience, and from sincere faith, from which some, having strayed, have turned aside.

1 Timothy 1:5

CHAPTER FIVE: *Integrity - Honesty with God and Others*

Here in this verse, we see that Love springs from three facets of integrity: a pure heart, a good conscience, and sincere faith. Typically, we tend to focus on the nouns as we read this verse: heart, conscience, and faith. But I would draw your attention to the adjectives Paul selects. He says Love comes out of a *pure* heart, a *good* conscience, and *sincere* faith. Pure, good, sincere: each of these adjectives reflects a different facet of integrity.

1. Pure Heart

If something is pure, it is not a mixture. Pure maple syrup is 100% a product of the maple tree, not an artificial concoction of sugar and flavouring. It is exactly what it claims to be. Similarly, a pure heart has nothing added in. There are no ingredients of deception or deceit. Walking with a pure heart means being just who you are without any pretense.

I used to curl in a Clergy Curling League. There was one pastor who would blame his bad shots on anything other than his own poor play. He would say, "The skip didn't give me enough ice," or "the rock picked up a broom bristle" or "the sweepers didn't start in time." It was never his fault. The man didn't realize that his attempts to be thought better of actually produced just the opposite effect. He was diminished in the eyes of others more by his words of pretense than his poor play ever would have.

Having a pure heart has to do with pure motives – there is no false front, no mask, no hidden agenda – you are just who you are. Integrity ensures that our words and actions come out of a pure heart.

2. Good Conscience

Our conscience protects our spiritual life. It warns us by making us uncomfortable when we are about to engage in an activity that will hurt our spiritual well-being. It acts like natural pain that warns us and causes us to pull our hand away from a hot stove that is about to injure us physically.

There are people who have lost their natural sense of pain. They have to be extremely careful because they can do much harm to themselves without knowing it. Similarly, our conscience must be in good working order and sensitive if it is to protect us. If we ignore it and continually override its warnings, we damage it and deaden its effect upon us. It is vitally important that we respond quickly to our conscience and not sear it by ignoring it.

A good conscience is one that has been heeded. It doesn't condemn you because you have responded to it. There is no lingering internal voice whispering, "What you are doing is wrong, you know you should stop, but you haven't." Integrity is having a good conscience and living up to all you know.

3. Sincere Faith

Sincere faith is a genuine, personal faith. It is not imposed by others; neither is it temporary. It is not a facade, or an outward expression lacking substance. Sincere faith is not a religious act. It is not an outward restraint keeping us in check; rather, sincere faith is an inner conviction that causes us to live our life in a certain way.

While a youth, I remember a friend saying to me, "Oh, I can't do that because it's against my religion." What the person was really saying was, "You know, I really would like to do it, and I want to do it, but I can't because my religion restricts me." His was not a sincere faith but an imposed faith. A sincere faith guides our behaviour and decision-making by what we really believe. Our actions are not determined by outward rules but by personal inner convictions that we follow regardless of who is watching or what others say or do.

CHAPTER FIVE: *Integrity - Honesty with God and Others*

Living in Integrity Means Being Perfect

Jesus discusses integrity at length in Matthew 5. In this passage, Jesus is delivering his Sermon on the Mount. He works His way through a list of commonly accepted behaviours and practices and shows His listeners how each of these understandings fall short of God's ideal. He then challenges them to strive for something more than they ever considered before – perfection.

> *You have heard it said, 'an eye for an eye and a tooth for a tooth'. But I tell you not to resist an evil person. But whoever slaps you on your right cheek, turn the other to him also. If anyone wants to sue you and take away your tunic, let him have your cloak also. And whoever compels you to go one mile, go with him two. Give to him who asks you, and from him who wants to borrow from you do not turn away.*
>
> Matt. 5:38-42

After laying down a brand new, radically different set of expectations for living, Jesus caps it all off with a bold, seemingly impossible statement in verse 48:

> *Therefore, you shall be perfect, just as your Father in Heaven is perfect.*
>
> Matt. 5:48

Jesus does not say "try to do your best" but rather He tells them to be perfect. This verse is really frightening! What does Jesus mean? If He is really saying that we have to reach the practical perfection of God, then we are in an impossible situation. An accurate understanding of Matthew 5:48 requires us to understand at least two things.

> *We exchange our life for His Life and His perfection becomes our perfection. We qualify for Heaven based on Christ's perfection.*

First, God's standard for entering Heaven and spending eternity with Him is perfection. Thankfully, we have that perfection in Christ Jesus. We take on His righteousness as a result of His death on the cross. We exchange our life for His Life and His perfection becomes our perfection. We qualify for Heaven based on Christ's perfection.

Secondly, the instruction of Jesus to be perfect happens in a very specific, focused context. Matthew 5 is all about how He wanted them to live in contrast to how the Pharisees lived. The Pharisees were focused on following outward regulations to the letter. Jesus was redirecting their attention to their inward attitude of heart. God wants us to embrace His perfection in our hearts and not just in outward actions. This perfection is not an impossible ideal, but something we can attain here on earth.

How is Perfection Possible?

Let's understand the second half of verse 48. If we are to be perfect as God is perfect, we must understand how and why God is perfect. God is perfect because He is holy. God's holiness comes out of His character; it is an extension of who He is. I heard a saying once that resonates with me: if you want to understand what "holy" is, put a "w" in front of it: "wholly." There is so much truth in this. God's holiness comes from being whole – without fault, without division, without error, without sin, without any falseness or deception. He is

CHAPTER FIVE: *Integrity - Honesty with God and Others*

consistent from circumference to core. He is the same yesterday, today, and forever. At the burning bush, God chose to identify Himself to Moses as 'I AM that I AM'. In other words, God says "I AM what I AM'.

God is consistent. He is whole. He is entire. He is complete. He can't choose to be good, since He is incapable of anything else. He IS good. He can't choose to be just, since He is incapable of anything else. He IS just. God acts out who He is.

This alignment between behaviour and character is called integrity. Wikipedia defines integrity as "the quality or state of being complete, whole, unbroken, unimpaired, perfect, sound, to be real, to be genuine."

> *God's holiness comes from being whole*
> *– without fault, without division,*
> *without error, without sin, without*
> *any falseness or deception.*

God embodies integrity, and we are to have integrity as He has integrity. In Matthew 5:48, Jesus commands us to emulate God's integrity. You and I are expected to be perfect in the sense that we are to move more and more toward being whole. We are expected to be who we are, to remove our pretenses and masks. We are expected to acknowledge the truth of who we are.

God's integrity manifested through us is sincerity and authenticity. It is being just who we are. We need to be the same whether we are alone or whether we are in a crowd. We need to be the same whether we are in the light or in the dark.

God is just who He is, and He wants us to be just who we are. When we are honest and acknowledge just who we are, we begin to move toward His Integrity. It is then that God is able to begin to transform us and make us into what He wants us to be.

We are called to be perfect in integrity as God is perfect in His integrity. There is no way we can be perfect as God is perfect in Heaven as far as an absolute standard of perfection is concerned. This sort of perfection is utterly impossible. Rather, we are to be perfect in the sense that we are moving more and more towards integrity. We are to be just who we are, take off all the masks, acknowledge who we are, admit our faults, and confess our sins.

When we go before God, we are to be honest with Him. Don't come trying to maintain some type of false front or image. Don't try to manipulate or bargain with God. Rather, we are to come with purity and sincerity.

Jesus told His followers a parable illustrating this in Luke 18. Here, Jesus describes a Pharisee who comes before God in the temple. He begins to pray, listing all the things he has been doing right, all of his good works: fasting, tithing, and so forth. At the same time, a tax-collector comes before God and takes a posture of complete humility. In sharp contrast to the Pharisee's prayer, he only mutters,

> *... God, be merciful to me a sinner!*
> *Luke 18:13*

Jesus declares that the prayer of the tax-collector, a morally repugnant man reviled by his peers, was heard over the Pharisee's prayer. Now, why would that be?

The Pharisee was certainly a better man as far as absolute standards. He was tithing, he was praying so many times a day. He was performing religious acts. Contrast this with the tax collector: he was a noted sinner, he was collaborating with the oppressive Roman government, he was extorting his own countrymen for financial gain. If you were looking for the better man, you would have to conclude it was the Pharisee. But if you were looking for the man who was the most honest and the most sincere before God, it was the tax collector.

> *When we are honest and acknowledge just who we are, we begin to move toward His Integrity.*

Simply put, the Pharisee was attempting to cover his sins and his faults with the list of good things that he had done, rather than acknowledging who he was on the inside. On the other hand, the tax collector was just completely honest. He took a stance of humility, acknowledged that he was a sinner and asked for mercy. And God heard his prayer over the Pharisee's prayer.

Integrity Connects with God's Heart

In Scripture, over and over again, Jesus spoke about integrity. In fact, it was one of His major criticisms of the Pharisees. The Pharisees were obsessed with the law. They scoured the complex Hebrew traditions, searching for loopholes and technicalities to exploit. They loved the law, not because it was from God, but because they could use it to control others. Jesus directly confronted the Pharisees' attempts to finesse and manipulate the law. He called them out on this behavior,

> *Woe to you, blind guides, who say, 'Whoever swears by the temple, it is nothing; but whoever swears by the gold of the temple, he is obliged to perform it.' Fools and blind! For which is greater, the gold or the temple that sanctifies the gold? And, 'Whoever swears by the altar, it is nothing; but whoever swears by the gift that is on it, he is obliged to perform it.'*
>
> Matthew 23:16-18

The Pharisees were saying if you swore by the temple or altar, your oath was not binding, but if you swore by the gold of the temple or the gift on the altar, then it was binding. God detests this kind of pickiness. Jesus tells them to just be honest and mean what you say. Have integrity, be who you truly are. Don't justify weaseling out of commitments by technical loopholes. He tells them to stand by their word: if you say 'yes', then mean yes. If you say 'no', then stand by it.

> *Let your yes mean yes, and your no mean no. Anything more than this comes from the evil one.*
>
> Matthew 5:37

Jesus calls us to complete honesty and sincerity. If we are going to express the Life of God, we must become more and more honest. This is the process of spiritual growth. This is the transition to perfection.

Living in integrity means that your actions are aligned with your knowledge. It means that you live out the things you know are right. But here is where we have a problem: we are human. We don't always do what we know we should. We fail and fall short.

CHAPTER FIVE: *Integrity - Honesty with God and Others*

How can we maintain integrity when we do not always do what we should? God has provided us a way. In order to maintain integrity when we fail, He tells us to be honest about our faults and acknowledge them to God and those around us. Living in integrity requires us to freely confess our sins to God and others.

> *If we are going to express the Life of God, we must become more and more honest. This is the process of spiritual growth. This is the transition to perfection.*

With openness and honesty, we confess our failures to God and ask for forgiveness. Like the tax-collector in Jesus' parable, we say "God, I have sinned, be merciful to me." Likewise, we are open and honest with those around us. Rather than hiding our mistakes and trying to maintain a faultless image we are to be honest about our struggles. You can maintain your integrity with God and others when you freely confess to them where you went wrong.

This brings us to our working definition of Integrity:

Integrity is living up to all that you know and, when failing to do so, freely confessing to God and others where you fall short.

Integrity is Our Handclasp with God

If you want to walk with God, you must walk with Him in integrity. Indeed, integrity is our handclasp with God – the means by which we maintain our contact with Him. To commune with God, we must be honest about who we are on the inside. But this goes against our natural instinct to cover up our faults and put on a good front before people.

> *You can maintain your integrity with God and others when you freely confess to them where you went wrong.*

Most of us minimize our known sins and cover our secret sins. The Pharisees and religious elite of Jesus' day were completely preoccupied with their status and appearance, and Jesus had harsh words for them:

> Woe to you, scribes and Pharisees, hypocrites! For you are like whitewashed tombs which indeed appear beautiful outwardly, but inside are full of dead men's bones and all uncleanness.
> Matthew 23:27

I grew up on a farm and I know from first-hand experience what it is like to whitewash the barn. If cattle are in the barn for any length of time, the walls can become splattered with grime and manure and they have to be cleaned. To do so, we would scrape down the walls to get the worst of the grime off. Then we would whitewash them. Whitewash is a watery, chalky lime solution, and we would spray it onto the walls, covering the filth with a white, clean-looking exterior. It looks surprisingly good even though it

CHAPTER FIVE: *Integrity - Honesty with God and Others*

masks a lot of dirt. Do not fall prey to the trap of image-management. The Pharisees did, and Jesus called them out as whitewashed tombs. They may have looked clean on the outside, but on the inside, they were full of corruption.

> *God wants us clean on the inside; the only way of accomplishing this is to be real, honest and sincere about the contents of our hearts.*

God wants us clean on the inside; the only way of accomplishing this is to be real, honest and sincere about the contents of our hearts. Notice how the Apostle John writes on this in his epistle.

> *This is the message which we have heard from Him and declare to you, that God is light and in Him is no darkness at all. If we say that we have fellowship with Him, and walk in darkness, we lie and do not practice the truth. But if we walk in the light as He is in the light, we have fellowship with one another, and the blood of Jesus Christ His Son cleanses us from all sin. If we say that we have no sin, we deceive ourselves, and the truth is not in us. If we confess our sins, He is faithful and just to forgive us our sin, and to cleanse us from all unrighteousness.*
> 1 John 1:5-9

God is faithful to forgive those who walk in the light and are honest about their sins. If you confess your sins, God is eager to forgive you, change you, and put His spirit within you. This honesty will allow you to continue to live a life of integrity in spite of your sins.

Paul was a man of integrity. When he was arrested and taken before the Sanhedrin, Paul defended himself by demonstrating his integrity.

> *Then Paul looking earnestly at the council said, 'Men and brethren, I have lived in all good conscience before God until this day.*
> *Acts 23:1*

Now that is quite a statement to make. I have lived in all good conscience before God right till now, there is nothing that is bothering my conscious. There is nothing in me that I feel I have done wrong which I have not made right. This is walking in integrity. What happens next underscores this all the more.

> *And the high priest, Ananias, commanded those who stood by him to strike him on the mouth. Then Paul said to him 'God will strike you, you whitewashed wall. For you sit to judge me according to the law, and you command me to be struck contrary to the law.*
> *Acts 23:2-3*

Highly educated, Paul knew the law; it was illegal for any judge to command guards to strike a prisoner. Immediately, Paul spoke up, pointing out his judge's lack of integrity: "You're judging me? You're commanding me to be struck? That's against the law." But notice what happens next.

> *And those who stood by said 'do you revile God's high priest?' then Paul said, 'I did not know brethren that he was the high*

priest. For it is written: You shall not speak evil of the ruler of your people.

Acts 23:4-5

Paul immediately apologized. He realized he should not have spoken that way to the High Priest, regardless of how the High Priest may have broken the law. Paul's conscience was sensitive; he realized his unwitting error and was quick to make things right.

> *I believe if we seek God with sincerity and integrity and then do what we think God wants us to do, we cannot go wrong.*

Integrity Guides Decision-Making

As a pastor, I come across many people who find themselves in difficult situations. They feel that their lives are off-track and at a dead-end. They have made bad decisions and now they don't know what to do. They are fearful that they may make another wrong choice that will make matters worse. In these times, there is a promise in God's Word that I share with them.

The integrity of the upright shall guide them.
Proverbs 11:3

This verse is a great comfort to anyone who is faced with a difficult decision and does not know what to do. It applies in everyday decisions as well. Perhaps you are considering buying a new home and there are two or three options before you. Strangely enough, there is no verse in the Bible that says "Buy the red brick bungalow on such and such a street." It is not there! But when you are faced with this kind of decision and you are not certain of God's direction, you can rest on this verse. If my choice is sincere and made with full integrity, God will guide me in that decision.

I believe if we seek God with sincerity and integrity and then do what we think God wants us to do, we cannot go wrong. If you are making the wrong decision, God will soon show you. He will turn the situation, or begin to work circumstances that clearly demonstrate the right way to go. On the other hand, if your choice was the right one, very soon a peace will come over you, and you will begin to find confirmations. You will feel, "Yes, I made the right decision." All of this comes as a result of your integrity.

The Protection of Integrity
We walk with God with the handclasp of integrity. You must maintain your integrity to walk with God. Integrity not only guides us but protects us. It protects us even when we don't know we need protection. But as soon as you let the handclasp of integrity go, and start doing something you know is wrong, you will find yourself in all kinds of difficulty. Many times, though, as you walk in integrity you may make a 'poor choice' just out of ignorance. You did not know any better. In these circumstances, you can trust that your integrity will protect you from the negative consequences of that choice.

Consider the story in Genesis 20, it recounts an incident that takes place between Abraham and a local king, King Abimelech. Now, in those days, it was fairly common for a local authority to forcibly remove a beautiful woman from a traveling company, kill her

CHAPTER FIVE: *Integrity - Honesty with God and Others*

husband, and take the newly widowed woman as his wife. Abraham was afraid of this happening to him, as his wife was very beautiful. To avoid this, he instructed his wife to tell people that she was his sister. Sure enough, as Abraham anticipated, King Abimelech inquires after Sarah, took her, and added her to his harem.

We walk with God with the handclasp of integrity.

Now after a short period of time, God appeared to King Abimelech in a dream and tells him that he is a dead man because he had taken another man's wife. Abimelech responded that Abraham said that she was his sister and he didn't know that she was married. He concludes by saying to God,

> *In the integrity of my heart and innocence of my hands, I have done this.*
>
> *Genesis 20:5*

Now pay attention closely to what God says to Abimelech,

> *Yes, I know that you did this in the integrity of your heart. For I also withheld you from sinning against Me; therefore I did not let you touch her.*
>
> *Genesis 20:6*

Now Abimelech may not have known why, but all the time that Sarah was in his harem, he had not called her to himself to sleep with her. God had protected Abimelech from sinning because of his integrity.

Do you see how powerful this is? If God would do this for a heathen king how much more will he do it for us. If you want to have God's direction and protection, walk in integrity. Always be honest, never be deceitful. Don't be underhanded. Don't connive in any way. Just be honest. Say what you believe. Live up to all you know. Walk in integrity.

If you want to have God's direction and protection, walk in integrity.

Integrity in your Words
Guard against technical justifications that destroy your integrity. Do you know that you can tell the truth and yet still be untruthful? We do so by selectively choosing some facts while omitting others in an effort to leave a false impression. We technically have told the truth but we have made a lie. Speaking a lie and making a lie are the same in the eyes of God and both destroy our integrity.

In this story, Abraham is guilty of this. Technically, Abraham told the truth; Sarah was his half-sister. While Abraham's claim was true, he did not say Sarah was his wife. No doubt, listeners filled in the blanks on their own, concluding that she must not be his wife since she was his sister.

If you're going to have integrity, you must be completely honest. There is no such thing as a little white lie. So many people justify lying and dishonesty by saying, "Well, it didn't hurt anybody ... I was actually lying for a good reason!" In your eyes, you may not have creat-

Chapter Five: *Integrity - Honesty with God and Others*

ed direct damage to another by your lie, but you have certainly damaged yourself and your own integrity. You need to draw a clear line and just always tell the truth. As soon as you are untruthful, you lose your integrity. You sear your conscience. When you walk in complete integrity, you are allowing this component of God's Life to manifest itself through you in a dynamic way. When you do, God promises to guide and protect you. You never need to be afraid of the truth.

Now, it is worth noting that integrity does NOT mean blurting out every thought that comes into your mind. Keeping your integrity is not at the expense of discretion. Having integrity does not mean that you have to speak every thought that you have about a person. No, many times it is wise to remain silent or to choose your words carefully. But when you do speak, you must communicate with full integrity.

My Early Experiences with Integrity

I clearly remember the first time my integrity was tested. I was six years old. Church had just finished, and as I walked down the aisle, I spotted a penny lying on the floor under a pew. I reached down and picked it up. As I did, I noticed a man sitting in the pew right next to me. Now he didn't see me pick up the penny and I thought to myself, "That penny probably belongs to that man. I should give it back to him." But then I looked at the penny, and I realized that the penny would buy me a bubble gum.

The internal struggle began. Should I put the penny in my pocket and spend it later or should I give it to the man sitting in the pew? I wrestled inside of my little six-year-old self. Finally, I decided to give it to the man. So I walked over to him and said, "This penny must be yours. It was on the floor." He looked at me and he said, "Oh no, you can keep it" and he put it in my hand. Jubilantly, I went off with a heart of integrity and a penny in my pocket. The bubble gum that I bought had no condemnation with it. I enjoyed it with a full heart of integrity.

If I had put the penny in my pocket, and later purchased and eaten the gum, I would have felt guilt. Guilt would have worked in my heart and produced a hardness as I either justified my actions or ignored the guilt. I am so glad that I acted in integrity that day; it protected my heart. I wish I could tell you that I have passed every test of integrity since then but I can't. That being said, my heart and my desire is to always walk in integrity.

As I sit here writing, a number of experiences from my youth come to mind. It is amazing how I remember them. They were tests of integrity that caused me to grow in Christ's Life and shaped my future.

I remember being in high school and receiving a test back and as I added up the marks down the column I realized the teacher had added wrong and had given me a higher grade than I deserved. I wrestled inside of myself. Should I go up and say something, or should I just say nothing and have the higher mark? Finally, I did go up to the teacher and upon rechecking she said, "Oh you're right, I did add wrong" and marked my paper lower. Now part of me wished she had said, "And I'll give you the extra marks for honesty" but she didn't. But it really didn't matter because I went back to my seat with my integrity intact.

Over and over, I've been tested along this line. I think we have all experienced getting change back and realizing we were given more money than we were owed. I have actually walked to the car and sat there and looked at the money in my hand with all kinds of reasoning going through my mind. "Well, they overcharge anyway so it doesn't really matter" or "they have insurance that covers this kind of thing and it is all worked into the price." It is amazing how creative our minds can be to justify dishonesty.

CHAPTER FIVE: *Integrity - Honesty with God and Others*

I remember one time walking back into the store and saying, "You know, you made a mistake here." And the person started to argue thinking they had given me less and I was wanting more money. I had to say, "No no, it's not that you didn't give me enough money, it's that you gave me too much and I owe you $5." She stood there and was just stunned that I had returned because I had been given too much. She couldn't believe that someone would return and actually give money back.

Even after this experience, sometimes when it happens I think, "Oh you know, it's not that much. It's not worth the trouble to go all the way back and make this right." I then ask myself this question, "Am I willing to sell my integrity for this amount of money?" And so I'll go back and make it right.

> *" I then ask myself this question, "Am I willing to sell my integrity for this amount of money?"*

Now I've told you some of the times when I was successful in maintaining my integrity. Let me share one when I wasn't so successful. Years ago I was selling a television and advertised it in the paper. But it was an older television and the tubes were going and it took several minutes before the picture appeared, but once it came on, it was fine. Someone came by and looked at it, and what I had done was turn the television on earlier so that when they arrived, it was already warmed up. I remember thinking to myself, "You know I probably should tell the person that it takes a while to warm up." But then I thought "Well, what difference does it make? It works" and I sold him the television. But you know, that has bothered me ever since. I was dishonest. There was something I was hiding. I was deceptive.

Shortly after I was married, I was traveling down to Tennessee by car. I was driving and going 10-15 miles over the speed limit as was my usual habit. I remember being convicted in my conscience that I was actually breaking the law by exceeding the speed limit. I wrestled with it for a while and finally took my foot off the accelerator and allowed the car to slow down to the speed limit. It is amazing to me how God will underline things for us. Kay, my wife, was sitting beside me in the car, and as soon as I took my foot off the accelerator and started to slow down she said "What's wrong? What are you slowing down for?" I realized that I had to tell her what I was thinking, so I did. Now that was important because, you see, the next time I was in the car and going over the speed limit, she said to me, "I thought God convicted you about speeding?" You know, God is really good to us in these things. He knew I was going to need that little bit of accountability she would give me, not once, but many times, right up until today.

When a man does something that he thinks is wrong – even if it really isn't – he breaks his integrity.

Paul's Teaching on Integrity

Now one of the places in the Scripture where we can gain more insight on Integrity is in Romans 14. Paul writes,

CHAPTER FIVE: *Integrity - Honesty with God and Others*

Receive one who is weak in the faith, but not to disputes over doubtful things. For one believes he may eat all things, but he who is weak eats only vegetables. Let not him who eats despise him who does not eat, and let not him who does not eat judge him who eats; for God has received him. Who are you to judge another's servant? To his own master he stands or falls. Indeed, he will be made to stand, for God is able to make him stand. One person esteems one day above another; another esteems every day alike. Let each be fully convinced in his own mind. He who observes the day, observes it to the Lord; and he who does not observe the day, to the Lord he does not observe it. He who eats, eats to the Lord, for he gives God thanks; and he who does not eat, to the Lord he does not eat, and gives God thanks.

Romans 14:1-6

Now here, Paul is talking about actions that Christians disagree on, whether they are sin or not, because Scripture is unclear about them. This is an interesting topic which could be discussed at length but I want you to see how this relates to the topic of integrity. Paul is saying when there is a questionable matter, let each person be convinced in his own mind and then let each person act out of integrity. He goes on to say,

I know and am convinced by the Lord Jesus that there is nothing unclean of itself; but to him who considers anything to be unclean, to him it is unclean.

Rom.14:14

Then he continues,

> *Do you have faith? Have it to yourself before God. Happy is he who does not condemn himself in what he approves. But he who doubts is condemned if he eats, because he does not eat from faith; for whatever is not from faith is sin.*
>
> Rom.14:22

Now let me explain what Paul is saying. In this passage, some Christians felt it was wrong to eat meat sold in the marketplace that had been offered to idols. Others felt that there was nothing wrong with this because idols were not real and they had asked God to bless the meat before they ate it. Paul makes the point that if a person believes it to be wrong and eats it, to him it is sin. If someone else does not believe that it is wrong, and eats, his behavior is not sin. Now, how can this be? Here are two people who do the same thing, to one it is a sin but to the other it is not. The answer is that one violated his integrity and the other did not. The sin wasn't in the eating but in the violation of his integrity. Remember? God's Life is shown through a pure heart, a good conscience, and sincere faith.

When a man does something that he thinks is wrong – even if it really isn't – he breaks his integrity. His heart isn't pure, his conscience is not clear and he is not behaving in accordance with sincere faith. Do you see how important this is? You must be honest with yourself and others, and align your behaviour with your faith.

Interestingly, at a later time, this same person may grow and gain more knowledge and understanding of Scripture and come to a different conclusion. Now he realizes that he was mistaken and the behavior that he thought was wrong is really not in the

CHAPTER FIVE: *Integrity - Honesty with God and Others*

eyes of God after all. Consequently, the same behavior that before was counted as a sin against him, now is not. You see it all depends on whether you are acting in integrity or not. Obviously, this only applies to questionable issues not to those that the Bible clearly defines as sin.

Reestablishing Fellowship with God

Many times I have talked to people who feel that God is distant and they no longer sense His presence. Now there may be several reasons for this, but one major cause I have found is that the person has lost their integrity. When this happens, how do you overcome the separation and reestablish fellowship with God again? Remember, integrity is your handclasp with God. What you need to do is go back to the point where you lost your integrity. Go back to where you did something you knew you should not have done. That is where you will find God. He is right at the point where you lost your integrity. To find Him again you need to approach Him with honesty. You have to own up to who you are and what you have done. When you approach with honesty and confession, God is there. He will forgive you. The relationship is reestablished and fellowship is restored.

Don't hide your faults nor keep your temptations secret.
Be open and transparent.

I must add that God has not actually left you, He will never leave or forsake His children. The separation you sense is a break in fellowship because you have lost your integrity. To regain the closeness, you must go back to the last point where you were in good standing with God, in purity of heart.

Again this is why the tax collector's prayer was heard and honoured and the Pharisee's prayer was rejected. The tax-collector was honest about who he was and asked for forgiveness while the Pharisee tried to hide all of his faults by reciting his good works. We just have to be honest. I really believe when we come before the Lord in prayer, one of the first things we have to do is just say, "God forgive me" and confess our wrongs.

> *When you don't live up to what you know you should, you will eventually suffer a breakdown in some way.*

A while ago I spoke to the leader of a denomination who told me about a time he had to deal with a pastor who unfortunately had fallen into sin and committed adultery. He asked the man, "How in the world did this ever happen?" The man shared that for the last two years he had been struggling with lustful fantasies and had lost his integrity in his thought life. Then as an opportunity presented itself, he fell into adultery. You see, this man had lost his integrity long before the physical act. Integrity is the only thing that will cause you to control your thought life. No one else knows what you are thinking but you. Lustful thoughts are only curbed by your personal integrity.

This pastor went on to say that he had not prayed for two years. But what did he mean? He was a pastor! He was in front of

Chapter Five: *Integrity - Honesty with God and Others*

a congregation and had prayed many prayers. But I understand what this man meant. If he really was going to pray and commune with God, the very first thing he would have had to do was to acknowledge the lust in his life and say, "Lord be merciful to me, a sinner." Someone looking on from the outside might wonder "How did this happen so suddenly? How did this man who led us in prayer every week fall into this horrendous sin?" But it wasn't sudden, it was a long process and the process started with the loss of his integrity.

Paul knew how important it was to walk in integrity and writes to Timothy, a young pastor,

> *Having faith and a good conscience, which some having rejected, concerning the faith have suffered shipwreck.*
> 1 Timothy 1:19

This pastor we were talking about suffered shipwreck. He ran amuck and aground. The danger is before all of us. But the shipwreck began with him rejecting his conscience. We have to keep our "faith and a good conscience." Don't hide your faults nor keep your temptations secret. Be open and transparent. As you maintain your integrity, you can stay the course, navigate temptation and arrive at your destination without shipwreck.

> *Every person who has been spiritually born again has an integral core within. To live with integrity, we need to draw upon this core and walk in the Spirit.*

We Cannot Live Without Integrity

You are not designed to live without integrity. You are created in the image of God and part of that image is integrity. When you don't live up to what you know you should, you will eventually suffer a breakdown in some way.

First, there is the spiritual breakdown that separates you from God. It then progresses to psychological breakdowns where you begin to feel stress, anxiety and depression and other negative consequences. Eventually, it culminates in physical difficulties. Your physical body becomes susceptible to headaches, ulcers, sleeplessness and many more devastating afflictions.

The ungodly way to cope with this is by medication or changing your world view. Your new philosophy justifies your present actions, and by doing so, you begin to convince yourself that the evil that you are doing is really not evil. And of course, the scripture warns us of this course and says that it leads to a reprobate mind. This is when a man can no longer discern between right and wrong because of the callousness of his heart. He has believed a lie.

> *...who exchanged the truth of God for the lie, and worshiped and served the creature rather than the Creator ...*
>
> *Rom.1:25*

This is something that we must avoid at all cost. There is a better way – acknowledge the Creator, confess your sin and walk in integrity.

Practical Steps to Establish and Maintain Integrity

1. Establish an Integral Core

This is what happens when we accept Christ. When we confess our sins to God and invite Him into our lives, He puts His Life within us through His Spirit. God's Spirit is always right, always honest, will always lead us and guide us in truth. As it says in 1 John,

> *Whoever has been born of God does not sin, for His seed remains in him; and he cannot sin, because he has been born of God.*
>
> *1 Jn.3:9*

This verse on the surface may seem hard to understand because we might ask ourselves, "Does this mean when I become a Christian, I will never sin?" Some people who have interpreted it this way feel great condemnation when they sin, and begin to doubt their salvation. But this is a wrong interpretation because earlier in the passage it tells us,

> *If we say that we have no sin, we deceive ourselves, and the truth is not in us. If we confess our sins, He is faithful and just to forgive us our sins and to cleanse us from all unrighteousness.*
>
> *1 Jn. 1:8-9*

So, even as Christians we will still sin, but 'His seed remains in us.' When we become a Christian, God puts His Spirit in our spirit, and one component of His Spirit is integrity. At the very core of our being, God places truth, honesty, and sincerity. God's Spirit has awakened our spirit, and we know in the depth of our being what is right. His Spirit in our spirit will never lead us wrong. It will always lead us to right thinking and actions. There is nothing inside, in our core, that will lead us to do evil. It cannot sin. Every person who has been spiritually born again has an integral core within. To live with integrity, we need to draw upon this core and walk in the Spirit.

I say then: walk in the Spirit, and you shall not fulfill the lust of the flesh.

Gal. 5:16

As we walk in the Spirit, we will by default avoid sin – and fulfill God's will for our lives. So step one, the very first thing, is to accept Christ as your Saviour. Just be honest and accept God and determine, 'I am going to walk out moment by moment what I feel in the innermost part of my being.'

2. Make an Air-tight Commitment to Integrity

You need to determine 'I will live up to everything that I know.' No exceptions. It has to be air-tight. When we talk about a ship and say that the hull has integrity, it means it is waterproof. There are no breaches in it. The hull of a ship can be 99% intact but if it has 1% holes, the ship will not stay afloat for long. It will eventually sink. The same is true of our spiritual lives.

We must have integrity in our thought life, not just our actions.

I came across these statistics a while ago and they really drive home this point:

If 99.9% were good enough, then:
- Two million documents will be lost this year by the IRS in the United States

CHAPTER FIVE: *Integrity - Honesty with God and Others*

- 22,000 checks will be deducted from the wrong bank accounts in the next sixty minutes
- 1,712 cell phone calls will be misplaced by telecommunication services every minute
- 12 babies will be given to the wrong parents each day
- 268,500 defective tires will be shipped this year
- 14,208 defective computers will be shipped this year
- 156,297 income tax returns will be processed incorrectly this year
- 2,488,200 books will be shipped in the next twelve months with the wrong cover
- Two plane landings daily at O'Hare International Airport in Chicago will be unsafe
- 400 pacemaker operations will be performed incorrectly this year
- 402 million incorrect drug prescriptions will be written in the next twelve months
- 18,322 pieces of mail will be mishandled in the next hour
- 315 entries in Webster's Dictionary of the English Language will turn out to be misspelled

So we can see 99.9% is not good enough. If you are going to have integrity, you cannot shoot for 99.9%. You must shoot for 100%. If a ship is going to have integrity in its hull, it has to be perfect – no holes. If a balloon is going to hold air, it has to have 100% integrity or it will deflate. If you are going to be a Christian, then you have to strive for 100% integrity.

So what is that last 0.1%? I believe it is our thoughts. We must have integrity in our thought life, not just our actions. Job speaks about this idea.

I have made a covenant with my eyes; why then should I look upon a young woman?

Job 31:1

Then he goes on:

Let me be weighed on honest scales, that God may know my integrity.

Job 31:6

This speaks especially to men because most temptations come to men through their eyes. To overcome like Job, a man must have integrity in how he looks upon a woman. He must make an agreement with his eyes as to where he will and will not focus. One man shared with me that when his vision fell upon some aspect that stirred his lust he would bounce his eyes. This is a practical application of making a covenant with your eyes.

> *If you are going to walk in full integrity, then the last .1% is controlling your thought life.*

There is a saying 'You can't stop a bird from flying over your head, but you can certainly stop it from building a nest in your hair.' So it is with thoughts of temptation. They are going to come to you – but that in and of itself is not sin. However, at that moment you are most vulnerable and you must be intentional in how you handle the thoughts.

You must not welcome lustful thoughts. You must not entertain them or dwell upon them. If you are going to walk in full integrity, then the last .1% is controlling your thought life.

3. Confess to God and Others Where You Fall Short

Integrity, then, is one hundred percent living up to all that you know. But as we have seen, none of us can continually do that. It is the goal that we all strive for, but we will fall short. Inevitably, we will all sin even when we know better. When this happens we can still maintain our integrity by immediately confessing to God and others where we fall short.

Obviously, the most important aspect is to confess our sins to God for He alone can provide us with forgiveness. Recall the earlier verse that assures us,

> *If we confess our sins, He is faithful and just to forgive us our sins and to cleanse us from all unrighteousness.*
>
> 1 John 1:9

When we sincerely turn to God and confess, He is faithful to forgive us and wipe our slates clean. But James writes and tells us that we also need to confess our sins to one another.

> *Confess your trespasses to one another, and pray for one another, that you may be healed. The effective, fervent prayer of a righteous man avails much.*
>
> James 5:16

This verse connects wholeness with confessing our faults one to the other. I have found over the years that when I try to hide my sins and keep them secret from others, I don't have much success in overcoming them. But when I confess them to someone else, it enables me to overcome. This is exactly what the book of Proverbs says,

> *He who covers his sins will not prosper, but whoever confesses and forsakes them will have mercy.*
>
> Proverbs 28:13

Many people have trouble forsaking their sins. They have sins that they are constantly confessing to God over and over again. They just don't seem to be able to let them go. I believe the secret to overcoming sin is found in this verse. The verse connects confessing and forsaking. Is it possible that the confession mentioned here is not only to God but also to others? I believe that it is. The main reason we hide our sin and not confess it to others is to preserve our pride. But by confessing to others, our pride is broken and the resulting humility makes us a candidate for God's Grace that enables us to depart from sin.

Sin thrives in darkness but when you expose it to the light it loses its power.

James writes,

> *God resists the proud but gives grace to the humble.*
>
> James 4:6

Chapter Five: *Integrity - Honesty with God and Others*

We may have confessed our sin to God, and that is good as far as forgiveness goes. But the key to forsaking a sin is confessing it to someone else. You must confess your fault to some other individual who you trust and who will pray with you and help you to live up to what you know you should do. This is so important. We really do need others to walk in integrity.

Ecclesiastes 4:9-10 says,

Two are better than one because they have a good reward for their labor. For if they fall, one will lift up his companion. But woe to him who is alone when he falls, for he has no one to help him up.

Eccl. 4:9-10

Here we see that we overcome with the aid of another person. You are not meant to do it on your own. We need the accountability and support of another person who is praying and encouraging us. Sin thrives in darkness but when you expose it to the light it loses its power. What is your deepest and darkest temptation, the one that you cannot seem to overcome? Someone needs to know what it is. Bring it to the light, confess it to someone. Pray and ask God to lead you to an accountability partner. My present accountability partner cuts right to the core many times when we get together. He just says, "Tell me what you don't want me to know." Now you do not need to confess your sins to everyone but you do need to confess your sins to someone.

Again listen to the wisdom of Proverbs,

He who covers his sins will not prosper, but whoever confesses and forsakes them will have mercy.

Proverbs 28:13

For many years I was part of an accountability group with three other pastors. We had regularly scheduled times that we met. Every time we came together we asked each other ten questions. It was humbling but also freeing to answer them honestly.

- Have you spent adequate time in Bible study and prayer?
- Have you been faithful in giving a tithe of your income to the church?
- Have you exposed yourself to any sexually explicit material?
- Have you given priority time to your family?
- Have you spoken negatively of any person?
- Have you related to a member of the same or opposite sex in any way that might be seen as compromising?
- Have any of your financial dealings lacked integrity?
- Have you hurt or been hurt by anyone?
- Have you fulfilled the responsibilities of your calling?
- Have you just lied to me?

We would go over these questions every time that we gathered together. And I can tell you that there were many times of confession, times of prayer, times of counsel, and they all worked for our benefit. Being part of a group like this has helped me to maintain my integrity over the years.

I encourage you to take the steps you need to walk in integrity. Why don't you right now take time to get alone with God and be honest and confess your faults to him – totally and completely. Then take the necessary steps to walk in integrity before God. Find an accountability partner, someone you trust who will listen to you, pray with you, and ask you the hard questions that will help you to keep your integrity. If we are to experience the abundant Life that

Jesus promised, we must be serious and draw upon this second aspect of God's L.I.F.E. – Integrity.

Understanding Love and Integrity and God's Judgment of Sin

Before we go on and look at the last two aspects of God's L.I.F.E. Let's take a moment and look at these first two aspects – Love and Integrity – and see how they relate to heaven and hell and God's judgment upon sin.

I have heard many people say, "How could a loving God send people to hell – a place of torment and punishment? If God is love, how could He do that?"

What they do not realize is that God is a God of Integrity just as much as He is a God of Love. God is just; that is part of His nature. It is part of who He is. Because of God's Integrity, every sin must be judged. Every wrong that is committed must be exposed and made right.

This is illustrated to us in the life of Cain,

> *Now Cain talked with Abel his brother; and it came to pass, when they were in the field, that Cain rose up against Abel his brother and killed him. Then the Lord said to Cain, "Where is Abel your brother?" He said, "I do not know. Am I my brother's keeper?" And He said, "What have you done? The voice of your brother's blood cries out to Me from the ground.*
> Gen.4:8-10

What was Abel's blood saying? I believe it was crying out to God saying, "Make it right. Make it right. I have been wronged. I have been killed. This must be made right."

> *Because of God's Integrity,*
> *every sin must be judged.*

God cannot sweep sin under the carpet. He cannot say, "I'll just forget about this. I know you sinned – I know you did an evil thing – but I will just forget about it." God is holy, He is just. If God could forget about sin, He would no longer be who He is, He would self-destruct. He is a God of integrity and when there is a wrong, His justice cries out that He must act to make it right.

How many injustices have taken place since that first murder? How many lies have been told? How many sins have been committed? Can you imagine the cry that must be in God's ears now after all these generations? The voices are all crying out in the ears of God saying, "Make it right. Make it right. Make it right."

God is God. He is who He is – and He will avenge every wrong, every injustice, every sin and make it right. To make it right, God's Integrity demanded that a just penalty be exacted for every sin. Scripture tells us what the penalty is.

In the Old Testament,

> *The soul who sins shall die …*
> *Ezekiel 18:20*

In the New Testament,

> *For the wages of sin is death …*
> *Romans 6:23*

CHAPTER FIVE: *Integrity - Honesty with God and Others*

But God's Love was not willing for man to perish so there had to be a way made to unite God's Love and God's Integrity. Love called for grace, mercy and peace. Integrity called for truth, justice, and righteousness.

God found a way to bring reconciliation. He sent Jesus.

For God so loved the world that He gave His only begotten Son, that whoever believes in Him should not perish but have everlasting life.

Jn.3:16

John 1:8 declares,

*And the Word became flesh and dwelt among us ... the only begotten of the Father, full of **grace** and **truth**.*

Jn.1:8 (Emphasis mine)

Jesus came to reveal both God's Integrity to truth and His Love's desire for grace. Jesus fulfilled an Old Testament prophecy in Psalms,

Mercy *and* **truth** *have met together;* **righteousness** *and* **peace** *have kissed.*

Ps.85:10 (Emphasis mine)

Jesus united God's mercy with His truth and brought peace with man in spite of the righteousness requirements of the law. How did He accomplish this? It was through the cross, where the God-Man hung between heaven and earth. The cross showed the righteous judgment of God upon sin as Jesus died for the sins of the world. But the cross also showed the Love of God for man as Jesus died in our place and bore the penalty of our sin that we may be spared. In Jesus, God satisfied both His Love and Integrity. He is the only way for this to be accomplished.

> *For there is no other name given under Heaven among men whereby we must be saved but the name of Jesus.*
>
> Acts 4:12

It is only because of what Christ accomplished on the cross that we are able to come into contact with God. Outside of Christ's payment, our sins will condemn us, and God's just penalty will fall on our own heads. This is why Jesus made His statement of exclusivity in the book of John:

> *I am the way the truth and the life. No man can come to the father except through me.*
>
> John 14:6

It is only when we are too proud or resistant to accept Christ's payment for our sins that God's judgment will fall upon us. In that situation, it is our sin that destroys us – not God.

> *In Jesus, God satisfied both His Love and Integrity. He is the only way for this to be accomplished.*

CHAPTER FIVE: *Integrity - Honesty with God and Others*

The True Reality of Hell

Consider a searing skillet on a stove top; liquid water cannot exist in the presence of the hot skillet. Should a water droplet fall onto the surface of the skillet, it would dance for a brief moment before "pssiff" – and it is gone. The red-hot pan did not decide to destroy the water. The water and the hot skillet are incompatible; the water droplet was destroyed simply because of the nature of things.

God doesn't send people to hell any more than a skillet decides to destroy the water. Simply put, our sin is incompatible with God. If we stand before a red hot holy God whose justice is absolute, we will not be able to withstand His presence. Even the tiniest shred of sin in our lives will destroy us because it is incompatible with God.

Sin will be judged; every wrong will be made right. The soul that sins will surely die. However, Scripture tells us that when we accept Christ, our life is hidden in Him.

> *... your life is hidden with Christ in God. When Christ who is our life appears, then you also will appear with Him in glory.*
>
> *Colossians 3:3-4*

Christ becomes our shield and protection. God, in His great Love, has provided a way of escape through Jesus Christ. Without accepting God's provision, however, there is no way we are going to be able to survive in His presence.

Imagine the futility of an egotistical drop of water that declares, "I don't need anything. I'm my own person. I don't need any help facing the skillet." It doesn't matter how macho the drop of water is, when it comes in contact with the skillet, it will be destroyed.

When we understand God's nature, specifically His Integrity, heaven and hell make sense. In the light of God's Integrity, we understand the vital importance of Jesus coming and bearing our sin upon the cross.

The Old Testament shows us clearly that God is just and righteous and every sin is going to be judged. The New Testament communicates and emphasizes God's grace. Since the death and resurrection of Jesus, God has been extending His hand of grace. If we will accept what Christ has done for us, we will be saved. But, grace makes no sense unless it is understood against the backdrop of God's justice and holiness.

Our life on earth is, essentially, a window of opportunity; if we accept Christ, our sins can be forgiven, and we are able to appear in the presence of God without fear of condemnation or judgment.

The scripture says,

Behold, now is the accepted time; behold, now is the day of salvation.

2 Corinthians 6:2

It is very important for us to see this distinction in God. He is loving, but He is also just. We must see that as strong and far-reaching that His Love is, His justice is just as strong and just as far-reaching. He does love the world so much that He gave His only begotten Son that whoever believes in Him will not perish, but have everlasting life. We do not want to stand in His presence and face the justice of God without the protection and insulation of Christ.

CHAPTER FIVE: *Integrity - Honesty with God and Others*

Notice how Paul expresses these same truths to the church at Corinth:

... God was in Christ reconciling the world to Himself, not imputing their trespasses to them, and has committed to us the word of reconciliation. Now then we are ambassadors for Christ as though God were pleading through us, we implore you on Christ's behalf, be reconciled to God. For he made him who knew no sin to be sin for us that we might become the righteousness of God in Him."

2 Corinthians 5:19-21

Paul explains, we have this ministry of telling you that Christ came and died for your sins so that you may be forgiven. If you accept it, you can be reconciled to God. When we are in Christ we are protected from judgment, and our sins are not held against us because Christ bore them on the cross.

When we are in Christ we are protected from judgment, and our sins are not held against us because Christ bore them on the cross.

The situation has not changed. These truths that were shared so long ago are just as valid today. Let me also add my voice and strongly urge you, if you have not done so, be reconciled to God through Jesus Christ and receive His Life.

CHAPTER
Six

Forgiveness - Without Qualifiers

To forgive is to set a prisoner free
and discover that the prisoner was you.

- Lewis B. Smedes

We are studying the four major aspects of Christ's L.I.F.E. – Love, Integrity, Forgiveness and Excellence – that provide the abundant Life that God desires for us to experience and express. As we come to this third aspect of Forgiveness, I cannot over-emphasize how important this quality is, and yet, how difficult it is to achieve. Certainly, the English poet, Alexander Pope, had it right when he wrote,

"To err is human, to forgive is divine."

Truly, to have this aspect of forgiveness, we need to draw on God's divine nature, His very Life. Otherwise, left to ourselves, every natural impulse within us wants to strike back in vengeance when we are wronged. Every internal drive wants to expose and punish our offender. Interestingly, when the roles are reversed, and we are the ones who have done the wrong, we just as strongly want to be forgiven and have the incident forgotten. We understand the importance of forgiveness for ourselves, but we lack the inward motivation and ability to express this same forgiveness to others. Obviously, we require a source of forgiveness outside of ourselves. So let's explore this third aspect of Christ's indwelling L.I.F.E. which provides the source.

Forgiveness was not only a major feature of Christ's life while on earth but the very reason He came into the world in the first place. Jesus came so that all mankind could be forgiven. Announcing the coming birth to Joseph, the angel said,

> *And she will bring forth a Son, and you shall call His name Jesus, for He will save His people from their sins."*
>
> Matthew 1:21

He came to save His people from their sins, remove the death penalty from us and give us eternal life.

One of the most familiar Scriptures in the Bible says,

> *For God so loved the world that He gave His only begotten Son, that whoever believes in Him should not perish but have everlasting life.*
>
> John 3:16

Many are acquainted with this verse, but not so much with the next verse which gives us the mindset of Christ as He accomplished His task.

CHAPTER SIX: *Forgiveness - Without Qualifiers*

For God did not send His Son into the world to condemn the world, but that the world through Him might be saved. He who believes in Him is not condemned, but He who does not believe is condemned already because he has not believed in the name of the only begotten Son of God.

John 3:17

When Jesus came into this world, He did not come with a message of condemnation. He did not come with judgment, but rather with a message of love, acceptance, and forgiveness. He did not come to straighten the world out but to make a way for it to be forgiven. Jesus was called a friend of sinners. How could this be? He was perfect, faultless and without sin and yet, sinners felt He was their friend. They felt comfortable in His presence. The reason for this was that in His presence they did not feel condemnation. What they did feel however was conviction. Condemnation causes us to harden our hearts and become defensive; conviction causes us to open our hearts and desire to change.

Condemnation causes us to harden our hearts and become defensive; conviction causes us to open our hearts and desire to change.

Today we are called to act in the same manner and show this same forgiveness. Just as God was manifest in Christ to reconcile the world to Himself, so we, as the body of Christ are called to the same ministry of reconciliation. Here is how Paul expressed it to the Christians at Corinth,

> *Now all things are of God, who has reconciled us to Himself through Jesus Christ, and has given us the ministry of reconciliation.*
>
> 2 Corinthians 5:18

We are to express and manifest God's Forgiveness to others. We are the continuation of the ministry of Jesus. We are living in a time of grace. The message of the church is one of forgiveness, not one of condemnation. The world is already condemned. Jesus did not have to speak a word to condemn the world; it was condemned already – rather He came to speak words of forgiveness. We are to manifest this same trait. We are to manifest forgiveness freely to everyone; to non-Christians, to fellow Christians, to members of our family, to everyone with whom we come into contact. This aspect of Forgiveness is so vitally important. We are exhorted in Colossians,

> *Therefore, as the elect of God, holy and beloved, turn on tender mercies, kindness, humility, meekness, long-suffering, bearing with one another and forgiving one another. If anyone has a complaint against another, even as Christ forgave you, so you also must do.*
>
> Col. 3:12

Now ask yourself, do you have a complaint against anyone? Do you have a grievance against your boss, a workmate, a classmate, a neighbor or your spouse? Has something been done to you; has someone misused you, spoken against you, ill-treated you? If you have a complaint, quite likely it is legitimate; you have truly been wronged in some way. When this happens, how should you react? What should you do? This verse says that as a Christian – "as the elect of God" – we are called to forgive. He is not expecting people who are not Christians to do this – they have no ability within themselves to do so. This is our calling, our response, our unique ability. This is the characteristic that we possess and it should come out in our words and actions. Furthermore, it is not just any kind of forgiveness, remember how the verse ends, "even as Christ forgave, so you also must do."

God has given us a standard of forgiveness to live up to, and that standard is the way that Christ forgave. Our expression of forgiveness is to be just like His. Now, no person can do this on his own. That is why God has placed this Forgiveness in our hearts by His Spirit. It is the third aspect of His L.I.F.E.

> *The message of the church is one of forgiveness, not one of condemnation.*

Now, some might excuse themselves thinking that the challenge to forgive as Christ forgave is extreme and limited in its scope. However, even a cursory study of the scripture shows that this is not the case but it is a central teaching and a distinguishing mark of a Christian. Let's look at another scripture,

> *And do not grieve the Holy Spirit of God by whom you were sealed for the day of redemption. Let all bitterness, wrath, anger, clamor, and evil-speaking be put away with all malice. And be kind to one another – tender hearted, forgiving one another, even as God in Christ forgave you.*
>
> *Ephesians 4:30-32*

This Scripture tells us that we should not grieve the Holy Spirit that is within us. We grieve the Holy Spirit when we react to the offense rather than following His leading to forgive it. Not only do we react with bitterness, wrath, anger, clamor, and evil-speaking; but we condone these feelings and actions. We think that they are only wrong when they are unjustified, but if I have truly been mistreated and wronged then they are appropriate. But this is not the way that Christ acted. Jesus lived a perfect sinless life, yet, many were still offended at Him and criticized Him. At His trial, when falsely accused, Jesus did not open His mouth but stood before His accusers silent. He did not defend Himself nor lash back in anger.

> *God has given us a standard of forgiveness to live up to, and that standard is the way that Christ forgives.*

However, this is not what we do. We justify our responses of anger and bitterness by feeling that we have a right to complain because the offense against us was so obviously wrong. But this Scripture is telling us that we are to forgive, even when the things done against us are truly unjust. We are not to react and complain – we are to forgive as Christ forgave.

How Did Christ Forgive?

So here is our standard: we are to forgive in the same way that Christ forgave. Now as this truth began to be impressed upon my heart, I asked myself the question, "How did Christ forgive?" To determine the

CHAPTER SIX: *Forgiveness - Without Qualifiers*

answer, I looked at the portions of Scripture where it refers to Jesus forgiving people and I was surprised at what I found. I started in Luke,

> *Now it happened on a certain day, as He was teaching, that there were Pharisees and teachers of the law sitting by, who had come out of every town of Galilee, Judea, and Jerusalem. And the power of the Lord was present to heal them. Then behold, men brought on a bed a man who was paralyzed, whom they sought to bring in and lay before Him. And when they could not find how they might bring him in, because of the crowd, they went up on the housetop and let him down with his bed through the tiling into the midst before Jesus. When He saw their faith, He said to him, "Man, your sins are forgiven you."*
>
> *Luke 5:17-20*

Notice that Jesus forgave this man's sin before the man asked for forgiveness. Even though the man had not acknowledged that he was a sinner or that he wanted forgiveness, Jesus offers the words, "your sins are forgiven you." Now, if this man was not very spiritual or if he did not understand how important it was for his sins to be forgiven, he could have said, "Well that's fine, but I'm still paralyzed here. I came for healing." But Jesus didn't heal him immediately – perhaps He knew that the man's greatest need was to be forgiven not healed. However, this was not lost on the people standing around, because the next verse says,

> *And the scribes and the Pharisees began to reason, saying, "Who is this who speaks blasphemies? Who can forgive sins but God alone?*
>
> *Luke 5:21*

> *It was strange how Jesus forgave this man. He forgave him before he had acknowledged his sin or asked for forgiveness.*

They really took offense that Jesus would forgive this man. Now Jesus, understanding their thoughts, responds to them – and He must have had a sense of humor because the way He responds is very interesting. He says,

> *Which is easier, to say, your sins are forgiven, or take up your bed and walk?*
>
> Luke 5:23

Jesus knew who He was. He was the Son of God. He was God manifest in the flesh. He had the power to forgive sins. Then He says to them all,

> *But that you may know that the Son of Man has power on earth to forgive sins"— He said to the man who was paralyzed, "I say to you, arise, take up your bed, and go to your house." Immediately he rose up before them, took up what he had been lying on, and departed to his own house, glorifying God. And they were all amazed, and they glorified God and were filled with fear, saying, "We have seen strange things today!"*
>
> Luke 5:24-26

CHAPTER SIX: *Forgiveness - Without Qualifiers*

Strange things indeed! It was strange how Jesus forgave this man. He forgave him before he had acknowledged his sin or asked for forgiveness.

Let's look at another example in John 8:3-11,

Then the scribes and Pharisees brought to Him a woman caught in adultery. And when they had set her in the midst, they said to Him, "Teacher, this woman was caught in adultery, in the very act. Now Moses, in the law, commanded us that such should be stoned. But what do You say?" This they said, testing Him, that they might have something of which to accuse Him. But Jesus stooped down and wrote on the ground with His finger, as though He did not hear. So when they continued asking Him, He raised Himself up and said to them, "He who is without sin among you, let him throw a stone at her first." And again He stooped down and wrote on the ground. Then those who heard it, being convicted by their conscience, went out one by one, beginning with the oldest even to the last. And Jesus was left alone, and the woman standing in the midst. When Jesus had raised Himself up and saw no one but the woman, He said to her, "Woman, where are those accusers of yours? Has no one condemned you?" She said, "No one, Lord." And Jesus said to her, "Neither do I condemn you; go and sin no more."

John 8:3-11

In other words, Jesus said, "I forgive you." Now notice the order in which Jesus said this. If it were me, I would have said, "Go and sin no more, and I will forgive you," but Jesus said it in just the opposite order. He said, "I don't condemn you. Go and sin no more."

Jesus forgave this woman before she acknowledged her sin, before she asked for forgiveness, and before she had changed. This is quite a standard that Jesus sets for us.

Let's look at another incident in Luke. Jesus is passing through Jericho and it says:

> *Now behold, there was a man named Zacchaeus who was a chief tax collector, and he was rich. And he sought to see who Jesus was, but could not because of the crowd, for he was of short stature. So he ran ahead and climbed up into a sycamore tree to see Him, for He was going to pass that way. And when Jesus came to the place, He looked up and saw him, and said to him, "Zacchaeus, make haste and come down, for today I must stay at your house."*
>
> Luke 19:2

Now by this act of going to Zacchaeus' home, Jesus showed His acceptance of the man. In a sense, He forgave him, although it is not spoken directly here. The whole demeanor of Jesus towards this man was not one of condemnation but of acceptance and forgiveness. Now again, this was not lost on the people who stood around because the Scripture says,

> *But when they saw it, they all complained, saying, "He has gone to be a guest with a man who is a sinner."*
>
> Luke 19:7

They thought, "How could Jesus do this? How could Jesus condone Zaccheus' behavior?" But He didn't. Jesus was righteousness personified and couldn't condone sin in any way. But He did show

CHAPTER SIX: *Forgiveness - Without Qualifiers*

His love, His acceptance, and His forgiveness towards this man. What was the result? We read it in the following verses,

> *Then Zacchaeus stood and said to the Lord, "Look, Lord, I give half of my goods to the poor; and if I have taken anything from anyone by false accusation, I restore fourfold." And Jesus said to him, "Today salvation has come to this house ...*
>
> Luke 19:8-9

Jesus' act of forgiveness towards Zacchaeus prompted a change in him; it produced repentance and salvation came to his house.

Jesus' act of forgiveness towards Zacchaeus prompted a change in him; it produced repentance and salvation came to his house.

Now let's look at one final incident at the end of Christ's life. After the soldiers had mocked and ridiculed Him and spat in His face and plucked out His beard and put a crown of thorns on His head, they finally nailed Him to the cross. On the cross he said,

> *"Father, forgive them ..."*
>
> Luke 23:34

Forgive them? They were still in the act of crucifying Him. These soldiers had not asked for forgiveness, they had not changed. He forgave them while they were still carrying out their sin. In fact, by being crucified, He not only died for the sins of the soldiers but for the sins of the whole world. The Scriptures state,

> *For the death that He died, He died to sin once for all ...*
> *Romans 6:10*

He died and gave Himself up so that everyone, everywhere could be forgiven.

So what do we learn from these incidences where Jesus forgave? He forgave the paralyzed man before he acknowledged his sin. He forgave the adulterous woman before she changed. He forgave Zaccheus who was a scoundrel and collaborator with the Roman government before he asked. He forgave the soldiers who were in the middle of crucifying Him and died for the sins of the whole world. Summarizing, Jesus forgave everybody, all the time, for everything, before they asked and before they changed. So if we are to forgive in the same way that Jesus did, our definition of forgiveness is,

God's Forgiveness is forgiving everybody, all the time, for everything, before they ask and before they change.

Now, this is a tall order and much more than what we may have ever considered in the past. Is this actually what Jesus meant? Peter seemed to have this question in mind when he came to Jesus and asked how far he should carry forgiveness.

> *Then Peter came to Him and said, "Lord, how often shall my brother sin against me, and I forgive him? Up to seven times?" Jesus said to him, "I do not say to you, up to seven times, but up to seventy times seven.*
> *Matt. 18:21-22*

CHAPTER SIX: *Forgiveness - Without Qualifiers*

I don't think we fully appreciate what Jesus said here. Peter asked if he should forgive seven times. Now Peter was not trying to set himself up to look unforgiving. When he suggested, "Up to seven times?" he thought he was being generous. Think about it.

A man sins by doing something against you, and then comes back and says, "Forgive me" and you forgive him. Then he does it again. After the second time, he comes again and says "Forgive me." You say "Okay, I forgive you." But then he sins against you again and for a third time he comes and asks for forgiveness.

I must tell you, after the third time, I think I would be a little reluctant. I would say, "Listen you've already asked twice. I'm not sure you're going to change. I'm not sure that you're sincere about all of this." So Peter may have thought this through and conjectured, "Well if I forgive three, four, five or six times, that's a lot of forgiveness. I'm pretty safe in asking the Lord if after the seventh time that would be enough?"

> *Forgiveness is something that is constant. It isn't determined by the circumstances or by the behavior of the person we are forgiving.*

But Jesus responded, "No, it's not seven times; it's seventy times seven." Peter may have thought, "Great, not only do I have to forgive, but now I have to do math." He may have calculated in his mind and said, "Okay, that is 490 times, so on the 491st time I don't have to forgive. No, we know that is not what Jesus meant. What Jesus was talking about was a perpetual attitude of forgiveness that has no limit. This forgiveness is something that is constant. It isn't determined by the circumstances or by the behavior of the person we are forgiving, nor is it optional. It is just always there. You forgive everybody, all the time, for everything. No matter what.

But What About Justice?
Now these are strong words, and I understand why some might have trouble with this. Is there not justice? Shouldn't people be held to account? Shouldn't there be consequences when someone does something wrong? If we just constantly forgive people, how will things ever be made right? These are good questions and the scripture addresses them,

> *Beloved, do not avenge yourselves, but rather give place to wrath; for it is written, "Vengeance is Mine, I will repay," says the Lord.*
>
> *Romans 12:19*

And in Hebrews,

> *For we know Him who said, "Vengeance is Mine, I will repay," says the Lord. And again, "The Lord will judge His people."*
>
> *Hebrews 10:30*

I don't need to judge and condemn because we know that every wrong will be exposed, every sin will come into the light. I do not have to judge because God is the judge, and He will judge justly. Now, if you do not believe in God or a judgment, then it makes perfect sense to pursue vengeance on your own. You had better get even because there will be no other redress. But if we

CHAPTER SIX: *Forgiveness - Without Qualifiers*

believe in God, we know that He is going to hold everyone accountable. He is the righteous judge and nothing will be missed or overlooked. Our assignment as Christians is not to judge or take vengeance but to forgive. We are not personally to avenge evil.

> *Our assignment as Christians is not to judge or take vengeance but to forgive. We are not personally to avenge evil.*

Some may say, "Okay, I see that, but shouldn't there be some kind of consequence of sin in this life? Shouldn't there be some kind of justice brought to bear upon wrongdoers in this world before the eternal judgment?" Yes, there is. The Scripture tells us that God has delegated authorities on earth who are charged with curbing the expansion of evil by exercising judgment.

> *Let every soul be subject to the governing authorities. For there is no authority except from God, and the authorities that exist are appointed by God. Therefore, whoever resists the authority resists the ordinance of God, and those who resist will bring judgment on themselves. For rulers are not a terror to good works, but to evil. Do you want to be unafraid of the authority? Do what is good, and you will have praise from the same. For he is God's minister to you for good. But if you do evil, be afraid; for he does not bear the sword in vain; for he is God's minister, an avenger to execute wrath on him who practices evil.*
>
> Rom. 13:1-4

There seems to be four structures of authority described in Scripture.

1. Government

God has ordained and recognizes national and local governments. They are charged with the responsibility to apprehend and punish wrongdoers.[28] When people break into homes and steal, we have the police force, people are arrested, they are brought before a judge and there is a penalty that is imposed.

2. Family

Parents are charged with raising their children in the fear and admonition of the Lord. They are to provide instruction and discipline. To teach and shape the lives of children, God instructs parents to discipline their children and impose appropriate consequences when their children do wrong. [29]

3. Social

Business owners, bosses, foremen, teachers, coaches, and those in other such positions have authority over the people who have entered into a social contract with them for some kind of remuneration or benefit. These authorities have a responsibility to see that the agreed upon responsibilities and tasks are carried out.

4. Church

There is a God-given authority in the Church. Leaders in the church are charged to exercise God's discipline upon members who sin. It

---

28. Romans 13:4;
29. Prov. 22:15;

CHAPTER SIX: *Forgiveness - Without Qualifiers*

is the responsibility of Church leaders to not allow members who blatantly sin in the congregation to bring reproach to the church by allowing their behavior to continue unaddressed.[30]

So there are institutions on earth where God's justice is carried out. The admonition to forgive is a command that is spoken to us personally. It is on a personal level that we are not to hold grudges or try to get even. Our personal mindset should be to forgive as Christ forgave –everybody, all the time, for everything, no matter what.

Now when we understand the depth of this teaching there are questions that automatically come to our minds. How can this be? If I forgive am I not just ignoring the wrong and the evil that has been done? Am I not condoning what has been done by forgiving? If I forgive where is the justice? Where will the correction come from? How will the situation be changed? If I just continually forgive, am I not just giving the person license to do more and more evil against me?

To our natural mind, all these questions speak against following God's command to forgive. But you know, just as in everything else, God's ways are above our ways[31] and our natural inclination can lead us to wrong conclusions. The Word of God shows us a better way to respond and still gain the desired results. Let's look at the example of how God dealt with our sin, restored us to fellowship and changed our behavior. I believe that this is the same pattern we should use to deal with those who sin against us.

As we have seen, sin is incompatible with God and is destructive – it ultimately brings the judgment of death. So when

---

30. Matt. 18:15-17;
31. Is. 55:9;

people sinned in the Old Testament God severely admonished them of the impending judgment. He gave ample cautions and warnings through His prophets calling upon the people to repent of their sins and change their ways. For the most part, the people ignored God's pleadings. When judgment did come, the people's repentance was short-lived and they quickly returned to their evil ways. There was no lasting change. The threat of judgment never altered their behavior. This was the pattern of the Old Testament. The world did not reform and it was moving to the final judgment. So what did God do? He found another way. He sent His Son, Jesus, to save His people from their sins. On the day Jesus was born in Bethlehem, angels appeared to shepherds in the field, and they proclaimed,

> *Glory to God in the highest, and on earth peace, goodwill toward men!*
>
> *Luke 2:14*

What did these words mean? Gloriously, God just unilaterally declared peace with man. In other words, He said, "I am no longer at war with you. I am no longer holding your iniquities against you. I have good will towards you. I am not going to bring my righteous vengeance against you. I forgive you." How could this be accomplished?

> *Then the angel said to them, "Do not be afraid, for behold, I bring you good tidings of great joy which will be to all people. For there is born to you this day in the city of David a Savior, who is Christ the Lord.*
>
> *Luke 2: 10-11.*

CHAPTER SIX: *Forgiveness - Without Qualifiers*

He could declare peace because born that day in Bethlehem was a Savior, who was Christ the Lord. On the cross God was going to pour out His righteous wrath against sin upon Jesus Christ rather than the people. Christ took our sin upon Himself and died in our place so that we could be forgiven.

> *The tool that breaks us, compels us, and produces the change in us is the Love of God. His forgiveness changes our hearts.*

Now by forgiving us, was God saying that our sin was of no consequence and we could just keep on sinning? Absolutely not. Paul addresses this exact issue when he asks,

> *What shall we say then? Shall we continue in sin that grace may abound? Certainly not! How shall we who died to sin live any longer in it?*
>
> Rom. 6:2

God's response was, certainly not. It is not God's purpose to perpetuate sin by removing all the consequences and penalties for it. But this is not the result of being forgiven. Notice what happens when He does forgive us – our hearts are gripped by God's grace and our stubbornness is broken. We begin to realize how deeply Christ loves us and receiving His forgiveness melts our hearts and causes us to truly repent. Paul writes,

> *For the love of Christ compels us …*
> *2 Corinthians 5:14*

The tool that breaks us, compels us, and produces the change in us is the Love of God. His forgiveness changes our hearts. The pronouncement of condemnation and the threat of judgment did not change us. But His mercy, His unfathomable love towards us, changes us. It is incredible. It is not our way – but it is God's way. Mercy triumphs over judgment[32]; it produces what judgment alone could never produce.

Forgiveness Causes Change More Than Anything Else

I am reminded of an old Aesop fable I learned in primary school, entitled, "The Wind and the Sun." The wind and the sun were talking one day about who was stronger. A traveler was walking down the street with a cloak on. Now the wind was quite proud of its strength and said to the sun, "Let's have a contest to see who can take the cloak off the man." The wind was thinking to himself, I'm strong, I can bend trees, I can go down and blow the cloak right off the man. What can the sun do? It's way up in the sky and can't do anything. Nonetheless, the sun accepted the challenge.

So the wind went first. He blew his hardest upon the man. The more he blew and the stronger the gusts that buffeted the man, the tighter he held on to his cloak. Finally, the wind just gave up. "No one can take the cloak off the man!", he declared.

Then the Sun said, "Let me try." The Sun shone his brightest upon the man and just bathed him with warmth. Suddenly the man began to unbuttoned his cloak and eventually took it off. The sun had won.

---

32. James 2:13;

Chapter Six: *Forgiveness - Without Qualifiers*

Although this is just a fable, there is real truth in it. The gusts of condemnation and cold judgment try to force us to change, but it only causes us to harden our heart and justify our sin, holding onto it all the more. However, the warmth and sunshine of God's love and mercy melts our cold heart and makes us want to do God's will. Not only does God shine upon us but He enters us and fills us with His Spirit.

This is how God accomplished our salvation and brought about change in us. This same course of action is what God calls His people to live out today on the earth. We are to unconditionally forgive as Christ forgave. Jesus taught,

> *You have heard that it was said, 'You shall love your neighbour and hate your enemy.' But I say to you, love your enemies, bless those who curse you, do good to those who hate you, and pray for those who spitefully use you and persecute you, that you may be sons of your Father in heaven ...*
>
> Mt. 5:43-45

Jesus taught this so that we might be like our Father in Heaven. If we carry out these admonitions, it will produce the results that the Father in Heaven desires. How are enemies going to be changed into friends? It is not by hating them – it is by loving them. How do we change people who hate us? It is not by condemning them, but by doing good to them. When someone is spitefully using us, we are called to pray for them – not a prayer that says "Lord, get them, Lord, bring judgment on them." – but a prayer that says, "Father, don't give them what they deserve. Bless them and shine favorably upon them." Contrary to our own natural thinking, this kind of love and forgiveness will do more to produce change in people than our pressure, revenge and retribution.

Look again at how Jesus forgave Zaccheus, a man who had betrayed his own people by robbing them and extorting money from them. Jesus shows acceptance by going to his house. Can you imagine this? The house Jesus entered was a house purchased by ill-gotten gains. The furniture He sat upon and the dishes He used were purchased at the expense of the people. But Jesus never condemned Zaccheus. He showed love and acceptance towards him, and what was the result? Zaccheus changed. Salvation came to his house. He said, "I'm going to give half my goods to the poor, and the things that I have taken from people falsely, I will restore fourfold." The change happened because of the love, acceptance and forgiveness that Jesus showed Zaccheus.

How do we change people who hate us? It is not by condemning them, but by doing good to them.

Do you believe that the same thing can happen today? Why don't you conduct a little personal experiment? The next time someone wrongs you, rather than reacting negatively, forgive them and see if it works like it did in the life of Jesus. Realize that you have received the Life of Christ within. Draw upon it and release His forgiveness through you. As you do, not only will you experience the inner peace of forgiveness, but you will have released the greatest power possible to bring about the change you desire in the person who offended you.

Don't feel that you cannot forgive until the offender repents or acknowledges that they were wrong. Remember that in these stories that we have examined, Jesus extended forgiveness before the people changed and it was His act of forgiveness that prompted the repentance in their hearts. If you condemn people, you will only cause them to be defensive, justify themselves and harden their hearts. But if you follow in the footsteps of Jesus and forgive, it will release conviction which softens the heart and brings about a genuine change in their behaviour.

Forgiveness Benefits the Forgiver
Not only does forgiveness benefit the offender but it benefits the forgiver as well. Forgiveness allows us to live our lives in peace. Do you realize that if you do not forgive as God wants you to, you will always be upset and agitated? You will weigh everything that happens to you on a scale of right and wrong and how it has adversely affected you. You will always feel abused and hard-done-by because there are more than enough injustices in life to cause this effect if you focus on them. You will live your life at a heightened level of stress and distress. You do not want to live this way. You want to live in peace, not turmoil. Listen to what Jesus said:

> *These things I have spoken to you, that in Me you may have peace. In the world you will have tribulation; but be of good cheer, I have overcome the world.*
> John 16:33

There will be tribulation in this world – just get used to it. Things are going to happen to you that are not right. You are going to be abused. You are going to be lied about. You are going to be cheated. You are going to be neglected. But Jesus says, "I have spoken these things to you so that you will have peace." Nothing will give more inner peace than letting the offense go and forgiving the one who wronged you. To live this out when bad things occur, you need to overcome your natural, negative response of whining, complaining and lashing back.

Peter addresses this very issue in his epistle,

> *Finally, all of you be of one mind, having compassion for one another; love as brothers, be tenderhearted, be courteous; not returning evil for evil or reviling for reviling, but on the contrary blessing, knowing that you were called to this, that you may inherit a blessing.*
>
> 1 Peter 3:8-9

This is our assignment – this is what we are called to do. Rather than rehearsing the wrong and reacting to the hurt, we are to act out of forgiveness expressing it in words and actions.

We do much damage to ourselves by rehearsing emotional hurts. Let me illustrate by sharing a time I was physically hurt a number of years ago. I was pulling a hose backward and accidentally stepped back off a retaining wall and fell four feet down, flat on my back. It knocked the wind out of me, strained my muscles and broke a number of ribs. For weeks I had to sleep upright in a chair and it was months before I fully recovered. After that, every time that I walked past the retaining wall, it sent shivers up my spine as I remembered falling off the wall onto the ground.

But what would you think if someone came up to me and said, "Oh, I heard that you hurt yourself and cracked your ribs." And I replied, "Yes, I sure did. Here let me show you how it happened." Then I proceeded to get a hose and pull it backward until I fell off the wall again onto my back. I mean, we cannot even image that.

Chapter Six: *Forgiveness - Without Qualifiers*

Why would I do that and go through all the pain again? I would just be reinjuring myself and deepening the hurt. Now, we would never think of doing this with physical hurts but we do it all the time with emotional hurts. We do not realize that because of the way that our inner psyche is constructed, every time we relive an emotional hurt in our mind we are inflicting the hurt all over again. Unaware of this, we continue to wound ourselves over and over again by replaying the video of the hurt in our mind and sharing it with others. By doing so, we are increasing the hurt and extending the damage.

What about you? When you are wronged and hurt in life, do you go over the memory of the hurt again and again? Do you relive the moment of shame, embarrassment or neglect? Do you rehearse the incident in your mind to see if perhaps you had missed some hurt that was intended? Do you share it with others and welcome their comments as to the wrongful behavior of your offender? If you do, you are unaware that you are climbing back up on that wall of offense and falling back down emotionally, deepening your hurt and hindering your healing.

Nothing will give more inner peace than letting the offense go and forgiving the one who wronged you.

Over the years, I have watched how some people react when they have been hurt. For the first day or two, it doesn't seem to affect them very much, and they begin to heal. But then they start thinking about it, and they replay the video of the incident over again in their mind. They go through the experience again and think, "Man, that really did hurt me. Why did she say that? She had no right to say that." Then they tell someone else about it and relive it again, and then on and on to others, again and again. Two or three weeks later they are crippled emotionally, overwrought and distressed. They attribute their condition to the initial wrong but it isn't – it is due to their replaying the hurt over and over in their mind. God's remedy for healing is forgiveness. It is as much for our good as it is for the person who offended us.

Yes, people will wrong you, but God is in control of your life. He is bigger than your hurt. He will compensate you. You will receive more blessing, far more benefits in your life when you trust in God and forgive rather than holding onto your hurt and trying to gain revenge. For your own good, you need to make a commitment to forgiveness.

Forgiveness is an Atmosphere

Forgiveness is not just an act; it is an atmosphere. An act of forgiveness happens when someone has wronged you at a particular time and you say to yourself, "All right, I will choose to forgive this person, this one time, for this offense." However, God doesn't want you to just live your life as a series of individual acts of forgiveness. He wants you to have an attitude of forgiveness, where it is not an event but an environment that you create around you. Whoever comes into your space – whoever comes into your environment – will find love, acceptance, and forgiveness. No matter what they do to you, you are not going to hold it against them. You will love. You will respond the way God wants you to – not the way that people treat you. Jesus taught that we are no better than sinners if we respond in kind.

> *And just as you want men to do to you, you also do to them likewise. But if you love those who love you, what credit is*

CHAPTER SIX: *Forgiveness - Without Qualifiers*

that to you? For even sinners love those who love them. And if you do good to those who do good to you, what credit is that to you? For even sinners do the same.

Luke 6:31-33

So we have seen so far that we are to forgive as Christ forgave and that Jesus forgave everyone, all the time, for everything, before they asked and before they changed. He had an attitude of forgiveness. This is a very high standard and we cannot live up to it on our own. It requires a manifestation of His Life from within us. It was said of Jesus that in Him was life and the life was the light of the world. And so it is with us. When we really understand what forgiveness is and allow Christ to forgive through us, we become the lights of the world that we are called to be.

> *Forgiveness is not just an act;*
> *it is an atmosphere.*

Forgiveness is Not Based on Merit

The first step is to understand how we have been forgiven by Christ and how little we merit it. He gave forgiveness to us freely and we are to offer it to others in the same manner. If we are of the mind that we have to earn our salvation by meeting certain standards, we will put these same standards on others. We will judge people and only accept them if they measure up. We can only forgive as Christ forgave when we understand that salvation is not by works but is a free gift that we receive through faith. The very best that we can do is insufficient. We can't earn it. If eternal judgment were based on merit, we would all deserve death. With this background, you can understand why it is preposterous for us to hope that people get what they deserve. If we do, we are asking that we get what we deserve.

Jesus gave a parable about a man who asked the king for mercy and was forgiven a great debt.[33] He went out and thereafter an individual came to him and asked for mercy for a far lesser debt. However, the forgiven man refused and cast his debtor into prison until he could pay all. When the King heard of it he called the man back in and said I forgave you – why didn't you forgive him? The king reinstated the debt and threw him into prison until the debt was paid. Jesus ended the parable by saying,

> *So My heavenly Father also will do to you if each of you, from his heart, does not forgive his brother his trespasses.*
>
> Matt. 18:35

God is serious about this issue of forgiveness. We must maintain an attitude of gratitude to God and extend it to others.

I have a pastor friend who told me a story about a breakfast he had with another man. This fellow always asked him difficult questions that seemed to have a twist to them. This particular day the man asked him, "Will drunkards go to heaven?" My friend thought about this for a moment and remembered the verse in Corinthians that says "drunkards will have no part of the kingdom of God."[34] So he thought he was on pretty safe ground and replied, "No, they won't."

The man said, "Wrong answer."

My pastor friend replied, "What do you mean wrong answer? The scriptures say that drunkards will have no part of the kingdom of God."

---

33. Matt. 18:23-34:
34. 1 Cor. 6:10;

CHAPTER SIX: *Forgiveness - Without Qualifiers*

And the man replied, "The right answer is 'I hope so.'"

Here is the attitude of forgiveness. Don't misunderstand, this attitude does not blur the edge of right and wrong nor does it remove righteous judgment. But it is an attitude that hopes that people do not get what they deserve. Will drunkards go to Heaven? A forgiving heart would respond, "I hope so."

> *Jesus laid down His life for sinners because He loved them. He hated sin and He hated what sin was doing to people. He gave His life to save His people from their sins.*

Can you imagine someone going to Heaven and really being ticked off? They look around and see someone that they just know in their mind has no right to be there. They think, "Where do I object? Where do I complain? I have to do something about this; there has been a mistake. They didn't work as hard as I did. They didn't believe what I believed. They didn't do what I did. They didn't sacrifice like I sacrificed to get here. Something is not right. I need to report this."

It is hard to imagine because someone who has been freely forgiven cannot hold this attitude toward others. Perhaps this is what Jesus meant when He said,

> *But if you do not forgive men their trespasses, neither will your Father forgive your trespasses.*
>
> Matt. 6:13

Jesus' statement was not so much a condition of forgiveness but a recognition that we cannot truly understand Christ's forgiveness and hold an attitude of unforgiveness towards others.

I am reminded of a story that Corrie ten Boom told about her sister, Betsie. Corrie and her sister were put into a Nazi concentration camp for hiding Jews and suffered greatly under the brutality of a certain guard. Corrie tells that one day, as she and her sister watched this guard beat another lady mercilessly, Betsie said, "Oh, the poor dear. How can we show her love?" Corrie wrote that she thought that her sister was referring to the lady who was being beaten. But then her sister went on to say, "I don't know how she could inflict such pain on someone else." Suddenly Corrie realized Betsie was talking about the guard. She was referring to the guard as the one who needed love. Somehow, Betsie saw past the brutality of the guard and felt compassion for her. She had freely forgiven the guard thinking, "What a victim this guard must be to have this kind of animosity and hatred in her heart that she could inflict such pain on a fellow human being and not feel any remorse." And so Corrie's sister referred to the guard as "the poor dear." Now this is the kind of heart God wants us to have – a heart of love and forgiveness. This is a heart that would lay down its life for others. Jesus laid down His life for sinners because He loved them. He hated sin and He hated what sin was doing to people. He gave His life to save His people from their sins.

A prayer is attributed to Saint Francis of Assisi,

Lord, make me an instrument of Your peace. Where there is hatred, let me sow love; where there is injury, pardon; where there is doubt, faith; where there is despair, hope; where there is darkness, light; where there is sadness, joy. O, Divine Master, grant that I may

CHAPTER SIX: *Forgiveness - Without Qualifiers*

not so much seek to be consoled as to console; to be understood as to understand; to be loved as to love; For it is in giving that we receive; it is in pardoning that we are pardoned; it is in dying that we are born again to eternal life.

This is the heart that God wants us to have. This is the heart of a person that God can use. He wants us to give His Forgiveness to others. To do so, we have to get past the wrongs done to us and think "How can I help the one who wronged me?"

Do you see it? Do you see the spirit that God wants us to have? This spirit of forgiveness hopes that people do not get what they deserve. We pray for them and ask God to allow us to manifest His Life to them. Jesus taught,

> *But I say to you who hear: Love your enemies, do good to those who hate you, bless those who curse you, and pray for those who spitefully use you. To him who strikes you on the one cheek, offer the other also. And from him who takes away your cloak, do not withhold your tunic either. But if you love those who love you, what credit is that to you? For even sinners love those who love them. And if you do good to those who do good to you, what credit is that to you? For even sinners do the same. Therefore, be merciful, just as your Father also is merciful.*
>
> *Luke 6:27-29, 32-36*

If we are Christians and are following in the footsteps of Christ, we are called to manifest His Life and allow His Forgiveness to flow freely through us. We will not act the way other people act. People in the world only love those who love them and only do good to those who do good to them. If we act in the same manner, what difference is there between us? In order to show the power of Christ's Forgiveness, we are called to forgive – even in the most adverse situations. This is a major trait of a Christian!

This teaching is so radical. You can imagine it must have shocked the people when Jesus first taught it. Resist not evil! Love your enemies! Bless those who curse you! Pray for those who spitefully use you! These words are still revolutionary to us today. They go against every fibre of our being, yet they are what we are called to follow. If we are going to show forth Christ's Life and follow in His footsteps, then this is the path we must walk.

The Path of Forgiveness over the Path of Condemnation

Are you aware that our assignment as Christians is to walk as Jesus walked? He walked the path of forgiveness not the path of condemnation. Jesus did not come to earth to condemn the world, it was already condemned. He came to save it.

The world is still condemned. Our job is to share the good news of forgiveness through Christ. We are not only to speak about it but to demonstrate it. We need to act in a way that people will sense that we love them, we care about them, and when they wrong us that we forgive them. Now, we can only do this as we maintain our connection to Christ and focus on our mission. When we know what we have been called to, we will not treat injustices as unwanted impositions, but as opportunities to be representatives of Christ. Otherwise, we will focus on the hurt and react. We will feel victimized and become resentful. Resentment, when undealt with, turns to bitterness which in turn grows to hatred. While counseling couples, I have heard one say to the other, "I hate you!" Now many may never say this out loud, but they too have harbored hatred in their hearts. Can you imagine? How contradictory is it for a Christian to have hatred in their heart

CHAPTER SIX: *Forgiveness - Without Qualifiers*

for someone else? This is not what God wants. God is a God of forgiveness and He wants us to have a heart of forgiveness.

We need to see clearly and take a good look at ourselves. If I am resentful and bitter towards someone, I need to realize that something is wrong in me. God does not want me to respond this way! But, do not try to respond properly in your own strength, it is beyond your ability. Press into God. Ask for His Spirit to come into your life and renew your mind and emotions. Experience His forgiveness and then pass it on to others. Show it by not giving people what you think they deserve.

> *When we know what we have been called to, we will not treat injustices as unwanted impositions, but as opportunities to be representatives of Christ.*

Separate the Offence from the Offender

One way to maintain this attitude is to realize that offenses will come. We should not think that something out of the ordinary has happened to us when they do. Peter writes,

> *Do not think it strange concerning the fiery trial which is to try you, as though some strange thing happened to you.*
> *1 Peter 4:12*

They are just a part of life – expect them. And when they happen to you, separate the offense from the offender. Love the sinner, but hate the sin. If not, you will put your hatred and loathing of the offense upon the offender, and this makes it extremely hard to forgive. The only way you are going to overcome the negative aspects of offenses is when you see that God is bigger than the offense and God loves the person who is offending you. He died for them. He has a plan and a purpose for their life. He cares desperately about them. He wants them to change. He wants them to come back into His order. The way that He is going to accomplish this is by using us, as Christians – the ones who are offended – as lights to show a better way. In the face of hatred, to show love; in the face of anger, to return a soft response. God wants us to show His Forgiveness through us so that people will change.

> *God wants us to show His Forgiveness through us so that people will change.*

God Works All Things Together for Good

A great example of how God can turn bad things that happen to us for good is in the life of Joseph. Joseph suffered a grave injustice by his brothers when they sold him as a slave down to Egypt. But Joseph did not allow this experience to taint him. When he was bought by Potiphar, he immediately began to serve and bless him in such a way that he rose to the position of chief steward in his household. Then Potiphar's wife lied against Joseph when he refused her sexual advances, and he was cast into prison. So now, because he maintained his integrity, Joseph finds himself in a dungeon – another great injustice! Remarkably, Joseph refuses to become bitter and maintains a good heart. He begins to serve the jailer, and he rises in the ranks of the jail until he can move from

CHAPTER SIX: *Forgiveness - Without Qualifiers*

cell to cell and minister to the needs of the different prisoners. He meets the Pharaoh's baker and butler who were imprisoned. He accurately interprets their dreams: the baker is executed but the butler is restored to the Pharaoh's house. He asks the butler to remember him and help gain his freedom but the butler forgets. Here again is an opportunity for Joseph to become bitter but nothing is recorded to that effect. After two years, the Pharaoh has a dream and the butler finally remembers Joseph. Joseph is brought out of prison, interprets the dream for Pharaoh, and as a result, he eventually rises to be second in command in Egypt under the Pharaoh.

All of this was able to happen because of Joseph's heart. He did not hold resentment and bitterness over anything that came his way. He put his trust in God, and even though things started bad and then got worse and then even worse, he maintained a clean heart – a heart of forgiveness. We know that this was the case because of how Joseph responded to his brothers who sold him into Egypt when they finally came before him. They realized that Joseph was now in complete command, and their fate was in his hands. They were so fearful that he was going to bring vengeance and have them killed. But listen to how Joseph responds to his brothers:

> *Then his brothers also went and fell down before his face, and they said, "Behold, we are your servants." Joseph said to them, "Do not be afraid, for am I in the place of God? But as for you, you meant evil against me; but God meant it for good, in order to bring it about as it is this day, to save many people alive. Now, therefore, do not be afraid; I will provide for you and your little ones." And he comforted them and spoke kindly to them.*
>
> *Genesis 50:18-21*

> *Do you know that if you love God and desire His purposes in your life, then all things will work together for good?*

Joseph was way before his time in understanding this aspect of forgiveness. He freely forgave his brothers. He said "I'm not in the place of God. I'm not going to bring vengeance and judgment against you. Yes, you meant it for evil but God meant it for good." God had turned all the evil against Joseph for good. This is a major key in being able to forgive the people who wrong you. You have to see that God is bigger than their offense. Even though there is evil done towards you, God is bigger and can work it all together for good. Paul writes,

> *And we know that all things work together for good to those who love God, to those who are the called according to His purpose.*
>
> Romans 8:28

Do you know this? Does this understanding permeate all of your thinking? Do you know that if you love God and desire His purposes in your life, then all things will work together for good? Not all things will be good, but all things will work together for good. You can relax, and you can forgive people. You don't have to feel that your entire future has been ruined. God is in control of your future. People can do evil things towards you, but they cannot disrupt God's plan and purpose for your life as long as you walk the same path that Joseph walked – a path of forgiveness; a path where you return good for evil; the path that Jesus walked.

CHAPTER SIX: *Forgiveness - Without Qualifiers*

I trust that you are excited about living out this aspect of the Life of Christ. Forgive as Christ forgave. He forgave everybody, all the time, for everything before they asked, and before they changed. He allowed His forgiveness to flow to everyone – in His life and in His death. Allow His forgiveness to flow through your life in the same manner. Living this way doesn't mean that we condone or pardon the sin of others. We allow God to be the judge. All we know is that God cares for and loves the individual who has hurt us as much as He loves us, and He wants to use us as instruments to inspire change in the person.

I came across this little four-line writing that really speaks to this. It is simply called Forgiveness.

> *Forgiveness is like the violet*
> *Sending forth its pure fragrance*
> *On the heel of the boot*
> *Of the one who crushed it.*

Sometimes we have crushing experiences in life. Someone, as it were, takes his or her heel and grinds it into us and we feel the pain. What fragrance do we leave on the heel of the boot of the one who stepped on us? God wants us to leave a beautiful fragrance – a fragrance of love, acceptance and forgiveness. We might think, "Won't I just become a doormat? I'm inviting people to walk all over me!" My experience has been just the opposite. Those who take this attitude, who have a humble heart, and do not hold onto the offense of those who wrong them, stand out and are admired as being strong. Their innocence and vulnerability actually increase their stature and cause them to stand head and shoulders above those who return evil in kind.

Let us rise above hurts and injustices and see the bigger picture. We are on assignment from God to show His Forgiveness. Let's allow His beautiful fragrance to come forth through us. I tell you, this will do more to motivate change in the people around you than the stench of your anger, bitterness, and vengeance.

All we know is that God cares for and loves the individual who has hurt us as much as He loves us, and He wants to use us as instruments to inspire change in the person.

CHAPTER
Seven

Excellence - A Godly Process

Excellence honours God and inspires people.
- Bill Hybels

My Dad was a dairy farmer but he also had a trucking business on the side. He would haul and deliver stone for individuals, local farmers and building contractors. He had an old truck that he had nursed along for quite a while. It still worked fairly well but it was getting quite rusty with holes developing in the fenders. Dad put off fixing them because money was short and he knew that he would eventually be getting a new truck. So he put up with less than the best. Finally, the old vehicle gave out and he bought a brand new truck, along with the latest hoist and box. As a boy, I remember being impressed when he brought it home, it was bright red with shiny chrome. Later, at the end of the year, after filling out his income tax return, I remember Dad saying, "I don't know why, but since I bought the new truck my business has doubled. I know nothing to account for it other than I have a new truck." I have never forgotten his words. Now looking back, I understand why his business increased. It was because the image of his business was transformed when people saw my Dad with his new truck. When they looked up and saw his truck coming down the road with his name and phone number on the side, they thought, "Let's get Miles to haul the stone. He has a good truck – he'll do a great job for us." I didn't realize it then, but I was seeing one of the benefits of excellence.

> *Excellence is a Godly quality because the Lord only does excellent things. He cannot do anything better than He already has.*

Excellence is the fourth aspect of God's L.I.F.E. that He wants us to experience and manifest. At first, we may question whether this quality should be included. To the casual eye, it seems to be superficial and even self-indulgent, not having the weight of the other aspects of God's L.I.F.E. But as we look deeper into this attribute you will see that it is an essential trait of Christ's character and one that God desires us to have and express.

Paul writes to the church at Philippi,

> *Being confident of this very thing, that he who has begun a good work in you will complete it until the day of Jesus Christ ... In this, I pray that your love may abound still more and more in knowledge and all discernment and that you may*

CHAPTER SEVEN: *Excellence - a Godly Process*

approve the things that are excellent that you may be sincere and without offense till the day of Christ.

Phil.1:6,9-10

In these verses, Paul prays that God would complete the good work that His Spirit had started in them. Among the good works He mentions are the three aspects that we have already talked about in this book. He prays that their "love may abound", that they may "be sincere" (integrity), and that they may be "without offense" (forgiveness). He then shares a fourth aspect that He wants them to demonstrate, and that is, "to approve the things that are excellent."

What does it mean to be excellent? Webster's Dictionary describes it as "superior in some quality, skill or achievement; surpassing."

This is certainly an aspect of God's Life, for the scriptures say,

He has done excellent things.
Isaiah 12:5

Praise Him for his mighty acts; praise him according to his excellent greatness.

Psalm 150:2

I think we can agree that all of the Lord's ways are surpassing; they are superior in quality and achievement. Excellence is a Godly quality because the Lord only does excellent things. He cannot do anything better than He already has. I believe this is why, when He looked at the world He had just created, He said that it was good. There was nothing more He could have done to make it better. God's good is excellent.

Paul says in Philippians,

Being confident of this very thing, that He who has begun a good work in you will complete it until the day of Jesus Christ.

Philippians 1:6

This good work is to produce love, integrity, and forgiveness in us, and now we see God wants to produce excellence as well. He wants to lift the quality of everything in our lives to the point that we only approve the things that are excellent.

If this is true, then let me ask you, "What do you approve?" What do you say is okay? What gets your stamp of acceptance? It should only be the things that are excellent, everything else should be rejected. But this is not the case with most of us. When we say something is "okay," we usually mean that it is not the best, it is not great, but it is passable, it's okay. But should it be okay when we are only to approve the things that are excellent? We need a new standard of approval. See yourself as a quality control inspector assessing the different areas of your life. What gets your okay? What kind of parent are you? What kind of spouse are you? What kind of work do you do? How do you keep your possessions? What do you approve? What is okay in your mind? The Bible tells us that we should only approve the things that are excellent. I think we really need a far greater appreciation of this aspect. If areas of our life are not reaching the standard of excellence, we need to look to God and improve them.

Excellence is a Godly Quality

Excellence is a quality of God – mediocrity is not. If we are going to manifest this aspect of His Life, we must fight mediocrity. We

CHAPTER SEVEN: *Excellence - a Godly Process*

have to reject the attitude that tolerates something that is less than the best. Mediocrity is not attractive. You do not see books for sale in the store entitled, 'How to Achieve Mediocrity', or 'How I Came to be Less than the Best'. These are not best-sellers because no one wants to be just average. Everyone inherently strives for something more. I believe we have this drive within us because we are made in the image of God, and He is excellent in all of His ways. He wants us to strive for the same standard and express excellence in our lives.

Some Christians react to this and while acknowledging that Excellence is a quality of God, they do not believe that we are meant to express it in our lives on earth. They assume it will lead to self-indulgence and extravagance. They ask, "Is it really spiritual to want to achieve and be the best? Did Jesus seek excellence?"

The answer is yes! Jesus modeled it for us. If you look at the life of Jesus, He was anything but self-indulgent and extravagant, but He did manifest the quality of excellence. At His birth, even though He was born in the humble environment of a stable and laid in a manger, the gifts He received were excellent gifts. They were gifts that were fit for a king: gold, frankincense and myrrh. Wise men were led by a star to travel a great distance to give Him these kingly and excellent gifts. Excellence was part of His birth experience.

Excellence is a quality of God –
mediocrity is not. If we are going to
manifest this aspect of His Life, we
must fight mediocrity.

If you look at the ministry of Jesus, He did excellent miracles. Turning the water into wine was an act of excellence within itself, but also the wine that He produced was described as the best that they had tasted at the feast.[35] Not only were His miracles excellent but the things that He possessed were excellent. Now, Jesus did not have much of this world's goods; in fact, when a man asked to follow Him, He said,

> *Foxes have holes and birds of the air have nests, but the Son of Man has nowhere to lay His head.*
>
> *Luke 9:58*

He did not accumulate many things in this life, but that which He did have, was marked by excellence. His robe was an excellent robe; it was seamless! At the cross, the soldiers esteemed its value so much that they gambled over it.[36] They all wanted His robe! It was an expensive robe. It was an excellent robe. Now, I'm sure that Jesus did not have a long wardrobe overflowing with robes – He was a simple and humble man, but the robe that He did possess was excellent.

Consider the anointing Jesus received before His death. When Mary came and broke the alabaster jar over His feet, it was an excellent anointing! In fact, it was so excellent, that when some disciples saw it, they complained,

> *Why was this fragrant oil wasted? For it might have been sold for more than three hundred denarii and given to the poor.*
>
> *Mark 14:4-5*

---

35. John 2:10;
36. Mark 15:24;

CHAPTER SEVEN: *Excellence - a Godly Process*

The scriptures say that it was worth over 300 denarii. In the economy of the day, it was about a year's wage. Mary broke an alabaster jar of oil on the feet of Jesus that was worth a whole year's income! Don't be too hard on the disciples, their motivation may not have been right, but there was some justification in their astonishment. In the face of their criticism, Jesus responded,

> *"Let her alone. Why do you trouble her? She has done a good work for Me ... She has come beforehand to anoint My body for burial.*
>
> Mark 14:6,8

Jesus welcomed and sanctioned her action, even while others thought it was extravagant due to the cost. Jesus made no apology for His excellent anointing.

Now let's look at the tomb in which Jesus was buried. It was a hand-hewn tomb. It was a rich man's tomb.[37] It was an excellent tomb. The life of Jesus, from birth to death, was marked by excellence. This is a quality of God's Life that Christ modeled and calls us to emulate. We are instructed to only approve the things that are excellent.

> *If you look at the life of Jesus, He was anything but self-indulgent and extravagant, but He did manifest the quality of excellence.*

---

[37]. Mark 15:43-46;

Excellence Distinguishes

If we are going to live our lives to a standard of excellence as Jesus did, it is worthwhile to see how this quality expressed itself in another character in the Bible. Excellence played a major role in the success and ministry of the Old Testament prophet, Daniel.

> *Then this Daniel distinguished himself above the governors and satraps because an excellent spirit was in him, and the king gave thought to setting him over the whole realm.*
>
> Daniel 6:3

Daniel stood out and was promoted because of his spirit of excellence. Indeed, excellence will distinguish you. On the contrary, there is nothing distinguishing about mediocrity – just being normal and average. If you want to stand head and shoulders above your peers and bring glory to God, then a spirit of excellence is required. It lifts you up and makes you visible. Jesus said that we are to shine like lights in this world. Excellence is essential in accomplishing this. Excellence is the feature that sticks out and gains attention. Excellence distinguishes. There were 120 satraps and three governors in Darius' realm and Daniel was so excellent that he stood out and was placed over them all.

Jesus said that we are to shine like lights in this world. Excellence is essential in accomplishing this. Excellence is the feature that sticks out and gains attention. Excellence distinguishes.

CHAPTER SEVEN: *Excellence - a Godly Process*

Years ago I read a book called, In Search of Excellence. It was written by Tom Peters and Robert Waterman. The book investigated America's greatest companies. Their criteria for greatness were companies that had longevity, had continual financial prosperity, and were marked by progress and innovation within their sphere. When they examined these companies, they found a single common characteristic – each one of them had a relentless pursuit of excellence. They wanted to be the best. They believed that they could and would be the leader in their field and they would not settle for anything less.

The authors said these companies were successful because they excelled in the basic fundamentals of business: quality, service, and reliability. Their success was not based on sleek advertising programs, a particular management technique, or some new product that caught a wave of popularity. It was because they just excelled in the basics. They didn't merely give lip service to them but actually practiced them. They really wanted their service and products to excel all others.

Excellence Values Quality

These successful companies pursued excellence to such an extent that some could say that they had an unjustifiable over-commitment to it. They just didn't talk about it, they pursued it with a passion. It was not only written down on a piece of paper, but it was the very philosophy of everyone in the company, from the president down to the lowliest employee. Their attitudes and actions were based on the driving pursuit of excellence. It was more important to them than their financial bottom line, even though it was ultimately enhanced.

Now, let me give you an example of a company that pursued excellence in the business world so that we can see the importance of pursuing it in our Christian lives. In the same way, excellence produced success for a natural enterprise, it can produce success for a spiritual purpose. The company is McDonald's. McDonald's is a phenomenally successful company, serving 68 million customers daily in 119 countries through more than 36,000 outlets. What do they sell? Hamburgers. Who would have thought back in 1955, a little roadside shack that sold hamburgers could become a multinational company that has so much influence around the world? What produced their ascendancy? I think it is safe to say that it was not their product, so what caused McDonalds to become so successful?

Authors Peters and Waterman discovered it was the philosophy of the founder, Ray Kroc. Every time he spoke, he focused on four fundamental values. He called them QSC&V: Quality, Service, Cleanliness, and Value. He never gave a talk or presentation without talking about QSC&V. Kroc did not just give lip service to these but his training manual spelled them out. McDonald's would give a quality product – Big Macs were to be thrown out if not purchased within ten minutes, french fries if not sold within seven minutes. They would provide quick service – they started the whole 'fast food' industry. Their establishments would be clean. I remember sitting in a McDonald's not too long ago, and watching the staff – it was a slow time – and as soon as the last customer was served in line, the teenage employees picked up cloths and began to wipe down the counter and mirrors. I thought to myself, "This is incredible. These teens wouldn't be doing this at home." But here in the store, they were going against their natural inclination and cleaning without being told. They were manifesting McDonald's third value of cleanliness. And finally, McDonald's fourth tenet, all their restaurants would provide value – people could purchase a good meal at a reasonable price without spending a lot of money.

CHAPTER SEVEN: *Excellence - a Godly Process*

The pursuit of excellence in these basic fundamentals have made McDonalds successful and world famous. Will not the pursuit of excellence in the basic fundamentals of the Christian life make Christians just as successful? We too are part of a great enterprise. It could be called, "God and Sons." It is the company of God's people. He has a plan and purpose for us here on earth. We are His representatives in this world. He wants us to be successful. We need to put the same energy, drive, and diligence towards the things of God that these natural companies have put towards their enterprise. They are working for a natural reward – we are working for an eternal reward.

What does our operating manual, the Bible, tell us about carrying out our activities on earth? There are two portions in Colossians that show us the way. They are a two-pronged encouragement to excellence. The first is,

And whatever you do in word or deed, do all in the name of the Lord Jesus, giving thanks to God the Father through Him.
Colossians 3:17

This first verse tells us that whatever we do, we are to do it in the name of the Lord Jesus. If you do something in someone's name, you are doing it on his behalf. God wants us to carry out an activity in such a way that when someone asks who did this, we can say Jesus. After an oil painting is finished, the artist signs his name on the bottom. The signature says, "Here is my name, I did this!" God is challenging us to do all that we do in such a way that we would not be embarrassed to sign His name on the bottom. So if someone asks, "Who wrote this paper?" We can say, "Jesus did." Who painted this house? Jesus did. Who cut this lawn? Jesus did. Who washed these dishes? Jesus did. Who did this job? Jesus did it.

> *Whatever you do, you need to realize that it reflects on the reputation of Christ – you are doing it on His behalf.*

This is a strong encouragement to excellence in our lives. Whatever you do, you need to realize that it reflects on the reputation of Christ – you are doing it on His behalf. When someone judges your work, they are really judging the work of Christ because He wants you to do it in His name.

The second portion of Scripture says,

> *And whatever you do, do it heartily, as to the Lord and not to men, knowing that from the Lord, you will receive the reward of the inheritance; for you serve the Lord Christ.*
> *Colossians 3:23-24*

These verses add an additional aspect. Not only are we doing it on behalf of Jesus but we are also to consider that we are doing it at His request, and He will reward us for it. In other words, when your boss asks you to do something at work, do not consider the request as coming from your boss, rather consider it as coming from Jesus. If you are a teenager, and your parents ask you to do something, do not think that you are doing it for them, rather regard it as something that the Lord has asked you to do. Think, I am doing this for Jesus.

Who should you be trying to please in your work? It is Jesus that you are trying to please. Rather than feeling imposed upon and taken advantage of, do your work as unto the Lord anticipating that from Him you will receive your reward.

CHAPTER SEVEN: *Excellence - a Godly Process*

Do you see the power of these two emphases? The first one informs us to do everything we undertake in His name as if Jesus were doing it. This attitude will lift the quality of our work. The second verse tells us to consider that everything we do is at His request, and He will reward us accordingly. This gives great motivation to our work as we realize that the most menial task that we undertake has an eternal significance and reward. These scriptures give us enormous encouragement to excellence. Considering all this, our working definition of excellence is:

Excellence is doing everything to the very best of your ability as unto the Lord.

Your best effort will appear when you realize that everything you do is ultimately for God. Notice I said everything, not just some things. Everything includes the way you keep your possessions? Do you keep them to excellence? Is your car clean? Your garage? Your closet? Your basement?

Embrace the mindset that things in your possession belong to God. He has given them into your care, and He expects you to keep them to the standard of excellence.

Whenever I teach about excellence, I feel challenged in my spirit. It is tempting to push the feeling of conviction aside as having no real consequence. Perhaps you too are thinking "Is excellence this important? Is it really what God expects? Are we not carrying this excellent thing a little too far?"

Let me share with you in all earnestness; I believe that excellence is of vital significance and a lost virtue in many Christian lives. Too many of us dismiss it as unimportant and unnecessary. Furthermore, I would suggest that excellence is the very quality that will allow the church to fulfill its calling to be salt and light in the world. Excellence distinguishes us and enables us to stand out.

Excellence is not just for the gifted few who have risen to the top by accomplishing great feats. No, excellence is a way of life for everyone regardless of their ability. The African–American educator, Booker T. Washington said,

Excellence is doing a common thing in an uncommon way.

Every Christian can attain excellence. Excellence is not living an extraordinary life, but living an ordinary life in an extraordinary way. We must embrace this truth in our day to day lives. It is interesting that Jesus said,

... for the children of this world are in their generation wiser than the children of light.
Luke 16:8

Unbelievers have learned the principles of excellence and applied them in the natural realm for profit. Meanwhile, Christians, for the most part, do not understand excellence. They haven't grasped the principles of excellence, their application, or their spiritual benefits.

I would suggest that excellence is the very quality that will allow the Church to fulfill its calling to be salt and light in the world.

CHAPTER SEVEN: *Excellence - a Godly Process*

> *Excellence is not living an*
> *extraordinary life, but living an*
> *ordinary life in an extraordinary way.*

I am calling for all Christians to lift the standard of excellence in every aspect of their lives. When you are doing something, ask yourself, could I do this better? Then, strive to do it to the very best of your ability. Why? You are doing it as unto the Lord, as His representative, for His approval in the end.

Now you may think that living up to this standard of excellence requires more effort and energy than you could ever maintain, and you would be right. But look at what the Scriptures have to say.

> *But we have this treasure in earthen vessels that the excellence of the power may be of God and not of us.*
> 2 Corinthians 4:7

Remember, you are not called to produce excellence through your effort alone. That kind of excellence is human and natural and can generate pride. The power of excellence is drawn from the treasure of God's Life within us. Every Christian has this Life within their earthen bodies.

Like the other attributes of L.I.F.E., excellence is impossible to generate outside of God's power.

Excellence Enhances your Self-image

As a Christian, you can look at yourself in one of two ways. You can see your earthen vessel or you can see the excellence of the power of God that is within you. I am challenging you to look at the excellence of the power within. Focusing there will give you confidence and faith to believe that you can do more than you ever imaged. Let God's power within determine your self-image, not your outward abilities.

A positive self-image increases your potential and causes you to believe for more. If you see yourself as a nobody with limited skills who cannot accomplish much, then you will act that way. How might your actions change when you see yourself the way God sees you? You will start behaving in an entirely different way! Paul seems to have grasped this reality when he said,

> *I can do all things through Christ who strengthens me.*
> *Philippians 4:13*

I am pushing you to see that you have a greater power within than you ever imagined, and in the strength of God's Spirit not to settle for anything less than excellence. I am referring to everything about you. It can start with the smallest thing – your handwriting. How do you write? I naturally have poor penmanship. If you were trying to read my notes, you would have a difficult time. In the past, I have shrugged it off and thought, "Of course, I can't write well – I'm a man. Men have poor fine muscle coordination." But truthfully, I have discovered that if I slow down and take more care, I can write well.

Let God's power within determine your self-image, not your outward abilities.

Now that may seem like a small thing, but I can tell you, that in the past, my sloppy writing affected my self-image. I was embarrassed to write a note because I did not want anyone to see my handwriting. I have found that by slowing down and writing my best as unto the Lord that I feel better about myself.

Excellence is Very Practical

Now let's get even more personal. Let's look at the area of your grooming. How do you look when you go out? What is the condition of your hair? What is the state of your clothes? When you walk down the street, do you look like you are a representative of Christ?

Many need to bring a new standard to the way they look and the condition of the clothes they wear. I have read studies that people work better when they have a better self-image. As you would expect, much of self-image is determined by what you see in the mirror. I am not speaking about physical attractiveness; I am talking about taking care of your body, which is the temple of the Holy Spirit. Look the best you can look. Comb your hair, brush your teeth, shine your shoes and make sure your clothes are presentable.

What about the quality of your clothes? You might think, "Well I don't have very much money so I can't afford to buy quality clothes." Don't fall for that excuse. You can look around and find bargains. You can find nice-looking, quality clothes for a reasonable price on sale. Quality is not more expensive. In fact, many times quality is less expensive. My wife and I raised four children. We did not have very much money when they were young and growing up. Sometimes we felt that we had to buy the most inexpensive clothing we could find for them. I remember buying a cheap pair of jeans for our toddler that only lasted a few weeks before holes appeared in the knees. So, we decided to buy a more expensive pair of jeans.

We bought first quality jeans and to our amazement not only did our first child wear them, but they were passed down to our second child and our third child and even to our fourth child. They lasted because they had excellent quality. We discovered that quality was cheaper than lower price in the long run.

Do not underestimate how your clothes make you feel. I am not just talking about a human pride, but about personal dignity, a feeling of respect that you have for yourself. I remember a statement that I heard a while back which was, 'quality is long remembered after low price is forgotten.'

> *'quality is long remembered after low price is forgotten.'*

We all have to live within our means and put limitations on what we purchase, but do not have the mistaken idea that buying the cheapest item is Godly. No, realize that you are a child of God, and it is not prideful to buy quality items. You are not self-indulgent or extravagant when you choose to live your life to a standard of excellence. As you do so with a right heart and attitude, you will find a growing respect for who you are in the eyes of God. As a result, you will look for God to manifest Himself through you in ever increasing ways.

Now this not only relates to the quality of the things you own but also to the care you take of them. What is the condition of your house? Does it need repair or cleaning? How do you care for your car? Does it need washing? God wants you to keep your possessions to the point of excellence. To do so is an expression of self-dignity and respect for God.

CHAPTER SEVEN: *Excellence - a Godly Process*

> *Don't allow shoddy or substandard work to diminish the attractiveness of your message.*

Years ago, I read a story about Charles Dickens' great classic, "A Tale of Two Cities." Dickens sent a manuscript of his new book to his friend who took it to bed with him to begin reading. After reading the first chapter, Dicken's friend got up, dressed, and went downstairs to his desk to continue reading. He felt that the excellence of the book deserved greater dignity and respect than to be read in bed, in his pajamas.

Is the story of your life so marked by excellence that it has the same effect on those around you? The Scripture declares that we are a letter written by Christ,

> *Clearly, you are an epistle of Christ, written not with ink but by the Spirit of the living God, not on tablets of stone but on tablets of flesh, that is, of the heart.*
>
> 2 Cor.3:3

God is expressing Himself through each and every Christian. Those around us are 'reading' us every day. It is important to realize that He is doing the writing, but we are the paper. We have seen that the Bible teaches that we have the treasure of God's Life in the earthen vessel of our body. First and foremost, this makes us realize that the source of the power is not from us but God, and He deserves all the glory. But it also makes us realize that His Life manifests through us. How we keep our earthen vessel and the things that it possesses is important. The standard is excellence. Do you see that this matter of excellence is not just a side issue? It is central to the manifestation of Christ's Life.

Don't allow shoddy or substandard work to diminish the attractiveness of your message. Embrace the attitude of excellence and present yourself in the very best way you can. Make sure there is nothing about your appearance, your possessions or work that detract from the image of Christ. Allow your light to so shine before men that they would see your good works and glorify your Father in Heaven. Remember excellence distinguishes, so let's be excellent!

A Few Examples from my Youth

I grew up in a small church with limited funds which required people to volunteer to maintain the building. Right next to the church was a house that the church owned. One day our pastor saw that the handrail on the porch of the house was loose and commented, "We're going to have to do something about that!" Now, there was a man in the congregation who heard this; I will call him Big Tom. He was a big-hearted fellow, so he came without anyone asking him, tore down the old classic handrail and built a strong new one out of "two by fours." When people came to church the next Sunday and saw it, they all looked puzzled at one another.

No one wanted to say anything to hurt Tom's feelings, but it just didn't look right. But what could you say? It was functional. It was solid. It was going to do the job, but it just wasn't excellent. It could have been made a whole lot better. The materials could have been better. The design of the railing could have been better. Big Tom had completed the job, but it wasn't excellent.

A little while later we were putting a connecting entranceway from that same house into our church building; the ceiling needed an overhead light installed. My brother and I walked in one day and saw that someone had indeed installed the light, but it was off-centre by about two feet.

To manifest the Life of God, we need to do everything to the standard of excellence.

My brother said to me, "Big Tom did this job, didn't he?" The job Tom did was very functional – the light lit up the room. It was just that every time you looked up, you would think, "Why didn't they put the fixture in the center of the ceiling?" It turns out there was no ceiling joist right there, and Tom didn't think it was important enough to go to the extra work to centre the light. He determined that since the extra effort required would not make a difference in the quality of the lighting, it was not worth it. What he missed, though, was the difference between a functional job and an excellent one. It detracted from the work and the appreciation that Tom deserved for his effort. Unfortunately, from that day till now, every time I see that kind of work, I think, "That's a Tom job."

To manifest the Life of God, we need to do everything to the standard of excellence. The standard should not be lowered due to cheaper cost or a lack of diligence. If we are sloppy and do half jobs lacking excellence, people will think less of us and our ministry.

Excellence versus Extravagance

Now, it is worthwhile to note the difference between excellence and extravagance. God does not want us to be extravagant, either by doing or spending that which is unnecessary. We are not to be extravagant; we are to be excellent. It is possible to cross the line from excellence to extravagance but most of us are more likely to cross the line from excellence to mediocrity. In fact, what many people call extravagant is really just what is necessary to produce the excellence that God desires. Remember, the disciples said the breaking of the alabaster box over Jesus' feet was a waste, but Jesus said it was appropriate. Many thought the act was extravagant, but it really was excellent.

What is appropriate? On vacation a few years ago, Kay and I visited the fashion capital of the world, Milan, in Italy. In the heart of their famous Galleria Mall, I found myself at an intersection. One corner was occupied by a high fashion fur shop, another corner by an haute couture dress salon and the third corner by a fine jewelry store. To my amazement, the other corner was a McDonalds. Where do you find McDonalds and other fast food restaurants? Not out on the back streets where the land is cheap. Rather, they are out on the commercial corners of the city.

McDonald's executives could have thought, "We can't afford to be on the main corner. We can buy property on the back street for a quarter of the price. Let's not be extravagant." This is not the mindset however of excellent companies. They realize that it is well worthwhile to spend the extra money for the prime pieces of commercial property that improve their image and exposure.

Four creatures are called "exceedingly wise." It could be said that they have a wisdom to exceed – to be excellent.

Chapter Seven: *Excellence - a Godly Process*

Now just think how this mentality could work in your life, in your family, in your home, in your business, in your place of employment, or in your church. We need to do things to excellence. So yes, be aware that you can cross the line into extravagance but be very careful that you have not drawn that line prematurely.

Others might suggest that this mindset is prideful and merely a justification for wanting to have the best. This would only be true if a person had a selfish spirit. But God has placed His Love in us, causing us to give generously to the needs of others. As long as our hearts are right and we know that we are pursuing excellence for His honor and glory, pride and self-indulgence will find no place in us. Through excellence, promote the kingdom of God, letting your light shine so that men will see your good works and glorify your Father in Heaven. If you are doing everything to the best of your ability as unto the Lord, you are going to hear Him say "Well done, good and faithful servant."

Christian Excellence is Exceedingly Wise

Proverbs, the book of wisdom, addresses excellence. It says,

> *There are four things which are little on the earth, but they are exceedingly wise: the ants are a people not strong, yet they prepare their food in the summer; the rock badgers are a feeble folk, yet they make their homes in the crags; the locusts have no king, yet they all advance in ranks; the spider skillfully grasps with its hands, and it is in kings' palaces.*
>
> *Prov.30:24-28*

Notice first in this portion, that four creatures are called "exceedingly wise." It could be said that they have a wisdom to exceed – to be excellent. The ant, the rock badger, the locust, and the spider are described as little and yet are given as examples for us to follow. Many people do not strive for excellence because they believe that they are insignificant. As a result, they assume that they cannot accomplish very much and certainly could not be the best at anything. This thinking is so wrong! Here in Proverbs we have the example of four small creatures that have a wisdom and philosophy that bring them to greatness. Their characteristics can teach us about excellence.

The Excellence of Ants

The ants are a people not strong, yet they prepare their food in the summer.

Proverbs 30:25

Ants work industriously all summer long storing food for the winter. They carry out this task even though there is no pressing need to do so. Their work allows them to lay up provision for the future when the supply will be non-existent. They do not put it off. They do not procrastinate.

The future is not pre-determined, it is shaped by what we do today. All the flowers of tomorrow are in the seeds of today.

The principle of excellence that we learn from the ant is:

Work Diligently Today to Prepare for Tomorrow

CHAPTER SEVEN: *Excellence - a Godly Process*

Solomon addresses the same point,

> *The hand of the diligent makes rich. He who gathers in summer is a wise son; he who sleeps in harvest is a son who causes shame.*
>
> Prov.10:4-5

Jesus, Himself, recognized the same truth,

> *I must work the works of Him who sent Me while it is day; the night is coming when no one can work.*
>
> John 9:4

We need to learn from the ant that right now, today, is the time to work. We need to overcome procrastination. There is an innate laziness in our nature that entices us to sit back and put off things until tomorrow. A simple truth that we must realize is "tomorrow never comes", because when it arrives, it is called today. Yesterday is just a memory and tomorrow is a dream – all we really have is today. The future is not pre-determined, it is shaped by what we do today. We will reap what we sow. All the flowers of tomorrow are in the seeds of today. The ant teaches us that we need to work diligently today. We cannot put this off. So many people dream of tomorrow but take no action today. They expect their future to take care of itself. Learn from the ant. Let's be what God wants us to be by starting today.

The Excellence of Badgers

> *The rock badgers are a feeble folk, yet they make their homes in the crags.*
>
> Proverbs 30:26

A badger digs. It burrows into the ground to make a refuge for itself. You would think that a badger would find the softest soil it could, in order to have an easy time digging. But this creature lives up to its name, it is a rock badger. He makes his home in the crags. When he digs it is not easy going. He hits rocks and has to tunnel up and around them or dig them out so he can make his burrow. He literally makes his home in the rocks.

The principle of excellence that we learn from the Rock Badger is:

Be Comfortable Going Through Hard Times

Jesus said,

... in Me you may have peace. In the world you will have tribulation; but be of good cheer, I have overcome the world.
John 16:33

In this life you will have tribulation, trouble and difficulties. It is just a given. Jesus never promised us an easy life. What He does promise, however, is that in the midst of the hard times, we can experience His peace, and that we can overcome because He has overcome the world. Like the rock badger, Jesus is saying that you can be comfortable going through hard times, so stop trying to avoid them. You might as well make your home there.

> *This is the confident attitude of the one who excels. He has a confidence that with God's help he can accomplish anything.*

CHAPTER SEVEN: *Excellence - a Godly Process*

The road to excellence is strewn with rocks.

So many people do not excel because they just give up in the face of difficulty. An obstacle stands in their way and they do not persevere. The little rock badger does just the opposite. Take on his attitude – keep digging until you see the breakthrough.

Calvin Coolidge said,

Nothing in the world can take the place of persistence. Talent will not. Nothing is more common than unsuccessful men with talent. Genius will not. Unrewarded genius is almost a proverb. Education will not. The world is full of educated derelicts. Persistence and determination alone are omnipotent.

The road to excellence is strewn with rocks. There are numerous obstacles along the way. We need to adopt the motto of the engineering corps of the US army which says,

The difficult we do immediately. The impossible takes a little bit longer.

This is the confident attitude of the one who excels. He has a confidence that with God's help he can accomplish anything. Do you exemplify that belief, or do you give up easily? Jesus said that He had overcome the world and all its problems. Realize that when something is too hard for you it is not too hard for God. Draw upon His Life within and persevere.

> *Christians should be the most confident*
> *and optimistic people there are,*
> *because we know the power*
> *of God's Life is within us.*

A member of our congregation told me not so long ago that he had taken on a role with significant responsibility in a major company and he was facing some complicated problems but did not know how to handle them. As a result, he said that he was spending a lot of time in the bathroom. When I looked at him puzzled, he smiled and continued, "Whenever I am stymied by a problem that seems insurmountable and I don't know how to proceed, I go to the bathroom and pray. I cry out to God and say, 'God I can't handle this. You put me in this position of authority in this company and it is beyond me. I'm asking for Your wisdom. I'm asking for Your strength. Show me the solution.' And it is remarkable! I come back out, sit down at my desk, and all of a sudden what I need to do comes to me. When I do it, it brings tremendous results." He concluded by saying, "Now, I'm getting all kinds of commendations from the CEO of the company and I almost feel sorry for receiving them – it wasn't me, it was the Lord giving me the answer."

Like the badger, this man found that with the Lord's help he could overcome problems that seemed overwhelming to him. So you too can relax in the comfort that God can energize your thoughts and mind and give you the insights that you need.

Christians should be the most confident and optimistic people there are, because we know the power of God's Life is within us. We can feel at home right in the middle of a hardship. We are not de-

CHAPTER SEVEN: *Excellence - a Godly Process*

terred or threatened by it. We know that if our lives are aligned with God's will, then His power will ultimately be displayed through us. The timing and results are in His hands.

Robert Schuller once said,

When faced with a mountain I will not quit! I will keep on striving until I climb over, find a pass through, tunnel underneath or simply stay and turn the mountain into a gold mine, with God's help!

Realize that while digging through a hard time, you may just discover gold. The scripture tells us to,

… glory in tribulations, knowing that tribulation produces perseverance; and perseverance, character; and character, hope. Now hope does not disappoint, because the love of God has been poured out in our hearts by the Holy Spirit who was given to us.
Romans 5:3-5

The problems you are going through are there for your benefit and will produce Godly character and love in you. I want to share a writing found hanging on the wall of Mother Teresa entitled, "Do It Anyway".

People are often unreasonable, illogical, and self-centered.
Forgive them anyway.

*If you are kind,
people may accuse you of selfish ulterior motives.*
Be kind anyway.

If you are successful,
you will win some false friends and some true enemies.
Succeed anyway.

If you are honest and frank,
people may cheat you.
Be honest and frank anyway.

What you spend years building,
someone could destroy overnight.
Build anyway.

If you find serenity and happiness,
they may be jealous.
Be happy anyway.

The good you do today,
people will often forget tomorrow.
Do good anyway.

Give the world the best you have,
and it may never be enough.
Give the best you've got anyway.

The problems you are going
through are there
for your benefit.

Let's take the lesson from the rock badger. Let's not be discouraged by the problems and the difficulties that come in our lives. Let's persevere and bring glory to God anyway.

You are not meant to achieve excellence on your own, you need other people around you.

The Excellence of Locusts

The locusts have no king, yet they all advance in ranks.
Prov.30:27

This third creature from Proverbs highlights the power of advancing together. When locusts move in swarms, nothing can stop them. When a swarm encounters a brook or stream or river, the first grasshoppers to reach the obstacle leap into the water, sacrificing themselves for the ranks behind, who cross over on their dead bodies. Farmers have set fires in the path of locusts to protect their crops, but discover that the fires are quickly extinguished by myriads of the dead insects as the countless armies march on. Tremendous havoc can be wreaked by a swarm of locusts, yet you can swat one locust away with your hand and be done with it. But when you have thousands of them together they can devour a countryside. They move forward without a leader. Instinctively they work not for the benefit of one but for the whole.

The principle of excellence that we learn from the Locusts is:

Committed People Working Together Can Produce
Amazing Results

Like the locusts, we need to work together to advance. To excel, we are going to have to do it with others. Reaching excellence on your own is impossible. God has designed it that you need the support and encouragement of other people around you. Remarkable strength is released when a group of individuals work together in unity. You are not meant to achieve excellence on your own, you need other people around you.

The Scripture says,

And let us not neglect our meeting together, as some people do, but encourage one another, especially now that the day of His return is drawing near.

Hebrews 10:25 (NLT)

There is something that happens when people meet together and work in unity. A synergy is produced – the whole becomes greater than the sum of its parts. Synergy is fascinating. Two boards that would support one hundred pounds each on their own, when placed together can carry considerably more than two hundred pounds. The added strength is the result of synergy. If you work on a project alone, you may be very talented and produce a good result. However, if two people work together, it will be even better, and three people working together will produce excellent results along with the added benefit of enthusiasm and excitement.

CHAPTER SEVEN: *Excellence - a Godly Process*

The analogies of the church in the Bible are always of a group, never individuals. The church is compared to a flock and no one sheep can be a flock. The body of Christ is likened to a body, and no one member can be a body. It is equated to a building but no one stone can be a building. It is described as an army but – despite what you see in Rambo movies – no one soldier can be an army. The church is individual members working together in unity as a whole.

Now how does this apply to you? To excel and reach your full spiritual potential you need to be part of a church – a functioning part, not just attending once in a while; or even regularly on Sundays. Being part of a church is more than your attendance. It requires knitting your life into the fabric of the church. Let your heart be joined with other members, and gain the strength and blessing that comes as a result. You know that you are indeed joined to the church when you carry someone's heart in your heart and they hold your heart in theirs.

> *You know that you are indeed joined to the church when you carry someone's heart in your heart.*

This principle applies in every area of your life. If you want to excel as a family, it happens by coming together and establishing family goals and working towards them. Doing this is exciting! When my children were young, I remember sitting down with them after supper and writing out our family values – what we felt and wanted our family to be. After discussing this for several weeks we finally agreed upon the wording of five values. We called them "The Miles Family Values," and had them printed out on parchment paper. Now, we did not always live up to them, but we certainly moved toward them. Today my four children are married with their own families but each of them still have their framed copy of our family values.

If you are in a business, or taking on a project, get together with other people of common interest who will work with you. There is a tremendous value in applying this principle in every area of your life. You can learn from others. I heard one man say, "If I have a dollar and you have a dollar, and we give our dollars to each other, we still each have one dollar. But, if I have an idea and you have an idea, and we give them to each other, now we each have two ideas." You never lose by sharing and helping others. The following is a story of how just one idea from a friend saved a business.

Years ago, there was a man who was a hairstylist. He was responsible for cutting and styling the hair of just about every resident in his little town. His income allowed him to live comfortably and even send all six of his children to college. Unfortunately for him, a big full-service hair franchise came to town and settled just across the street from his little salon. Immediately it began a media campaign: signs on its windows and ads in the newspaper announced, "Everything for $10.00! $10.00 haircuts, $10.00 perms. Everything for $10.00!" Soon all of his customers began visiting the shop across the street and the man's business sat empty. Desperate, he called a friend over and told him his story, "I'm finished! It's impossible for me to compete against them!" His friend squinted his eyes at the salon across the street and told him, "I have an idea." He picked up the phone and dialed the town's only billboard company. "Yes, right on top of our salon, big letters … The message? … We fix $10.00 haircuts."

CHAPTER SEVEN: *Excellence - a Godly Process*

The Excellence of Spiders

The spider skillfully grasps with its hands and is in King's palaces.

Prov. 30:28

I like the translations of the Bible that render the fourth creature as a spider. It speaks to the point that a spider is adept at moving forward hand over hand on the thread that it spins. Even though most people want to get rid of spiders by removing all the cobwebs that they can find, these creatures still have figured out a way to overcome and prevail. They are everywhere – not only in poor men's cottages but in King's palaces as well. They have reached the highest places by skillfully grasping, spinning and using what is in their hands.

The principle of excellence that we learn from the spider is:

Be Adept at Using What is in your Hand Right Now

Have you ever watched a spider drop down from the ceiling on a thread and then climb back up again, spinning its web? It grasps the thread hand over hand and can jump, move, maneuver from one place to another, just following the fine threads that it has spun. Now what is the lesson the Lord is trying to teach us in this verse? It is this: if we are going to reach the height of our full potential, we do so by skillfully handling what is in our hands today. We do it hand over hand over hand. We start with what we have now and manage it deftly and competently. As we do so, it will lead us to the next hand grasp of opportunity. Handling it successfully will give rise to the next thing and the next thing. Through this progression, we will find that we are on a journey to the King's palace. We will reach the heights of our full potential and fulfill God's will for our lives.

So many people fail to advance because they are always looking for their big break. They have responsibility now but they dismiss it as inconsequential and give little attention to their work. As a result, their production is poor or just average. They think if someone could just see their potential and provide them with a break, then they would really shine. But the way to excellence is to start right now where you are, with whatever is in your hand, and work skillfully as unto the Lord.

Jesus gives this insight,

> *The one who is faithful in a very little is also faithful in much, and the one who is dishonest in a very little is also dishonest in much. If then you haven't been trustworthy in handling worldly wealth, who will entrust you with the true riches? And if you haven't been trustworthy with someone else's property, who will give you your own?*
>
> Luke 16:10-12

If you want to grow and succeed, you have to be faithful in the little things and as you handle them well, God will give you more.

When God called Moses to lead the children of Israel out of Egypt, He asked him a question,

> *"What is that in your hand?" He said, "A rod." And He said, "Cast it on the ground." So he cast it on the ground, and it became a serpent; and Moses fled from it. Then the Lord said to Moses, "Reach out your hand and take it by the tail" and*

he reached out his hand and caught it, and it became a rod in his hand.

Exodus 4:2-4

This is symbolic of what God wants you to do with what is in your hand. He first asks you to throw it down and yield it to Him. When you do, for the first time you see its serpent-like qualities. The thing that you were using for your own benefit and glory has the potential to be an instrument that Satan could use to control your thoughts and actions. Any particular ability or talent that has not been submitted to the Lord has the ability, like a serpent, to turn and bite you. But if you offer it to the Lord, He sanctifies it and has you pick it back up again. Now you do your job or task using your talents and abilities as unto the Lord. Notice, from the time that Moses cast down his rod and picked it back up again, it was no longer called the rod of Moses but the rod of the Lord. Moses held the rod over the Red Sea, and it parted, he struck the rock with it and water came forth. God allowed Moses to use the rod for the remainder of his ministry as an instrument to release His power. That which is in your hand has the same potential to achieve great and excellent things when yielded to God.

---

*If we are going to be excellent,
then we need to skillfully handle
what is in our hands, doing everything
to the very best of our ability
as unto the Lord*

Let me ask you the same question that God asked Moses: What is in your hand? Is it a pencil? Is it a hammer? Is it a computer? Is it a lathe? Is it a steering wheel? What is it that you are using? What is in your hand? I would encourage you to turn it over to the Lord, and then use it skillfully for His glory.

This is very powerful to us today. If we are going to be excellent, then we need to skillfully handle what is in our hands, doing everything to the very best of our ability as unto the Lord. As we use what we have for the glory of God, we are going to reach the King's palace.

Christian Excellence Exceeds Expectations

A distinguishing mark of excellence is that it exceeds expectations. You can do something well but if it does not exceed people's expectation it still falls short of excellence. Jesus spoke about this in His sermon on the mount. He taught,

> *But whoever slaps you on your right cheek, turn the other to him also. If anyone wants to sue you and take away your tunic, let him have your cloak also. And whoever compels you to go one mile, go with him two.*
>
> *Matthew 5:39-41*

Here, Jesus gives three examples teaching how to exceed expectations. First, if someone hits you on the right cheek you should turn to him the left. This is not the typical reaction. The usual response is to hit him back. A good person might restrain his desire to hit back and bear the injury without responding in kind. By behaving this way, we think we have acted Godly by just letting the injury go. But Jesus did not just teach to not hit back, he tells us to turn the other cheek. This exceeds what we or others would expect. We are not just to ignore

CHAPTER SEVEN: *Excellence - a Godly Process*

the hurt but we are to stay open to further hurt. You do realize here that Jesus is not just speaking of physical slaps, but of emotional slaps as well, which come as the result of the hurtful words and actions of others. We are to stand out in this world by not only refusing to answer back, but by maintaining the relationship. We remain vulnerable and refuse to withdraw.

A distinguishing mark of excellence is that it exceeds expectations.

Then he goes on and teaches what you should do when someone sues you at court and takes away your tunic. The typical reaction is to fight back and launch a countersuit to retrieve your tunic. We expect that the Christian response is to not countersue, but to gracefully give up our tunic. But Jesus says, "Give them your cloak also." The Lord knows that if we just refrain from countersuing, we are not actually making a difference. We are not distinguishing ourselves, we are not excelling. We are just doing what people think a good person should do.

The final example that Jesus gives is when you are forced to go a mile. Apparently, a Roman soldier could commandeer a citizen to carry his gear for a mile. When this happened, a person may be tempted to run away. The standard expectation is that a good person would submit and go the mile without complaint. Jesus again teaches something more. He says that we should go an extra mile. This exceeds by a mile (excuse the pun) what the average expectation would be. Christians most of the time just do not go far enough. It is only when we go beyond expectations that we find the power and blessing of excellence portrayed.

> *Many times we don't experience the results that we want because we just do not go far enough. We stop short of the principle of excellence.*

There is a story that Watchman Nee, a Chinese Christian, tells in one of his books. Two Christian brothers were farmers. They had a rice paddy that needed to be irrigated. Their paddy was halfway up a hill while others were below. During the day, they would draw water and fill their paddy. One night, an unscrupulous farmer below them dug a hole in their rice paddy wall and drained the water into his field. Being Christians, they felt that they should suffer wrong without complaint, so they repaired the dyke and drew water for their paddy again. However, the same thing happened over the next several days. They continued to do what they felt was right, even though others suggested that they stand guard to catch and beat the one doing it. In spite of their Godly stance, they lacked peace and felt frustrated that nothing had changed. They went to their pastor and asked him what they should do. He said that they were not going far enough. He advised them to draw water for their neighbour's paddy and then draw water for their own. After doing this, they felt an inner peace and a few days later, the person who had stolen the water came with a broken heart to apologize, saying, "If this is Christianity, I want to hear about it."

Many times we don't experience the results that we want because we just do not go far enough. We stop short of the principle of excellence. Let's be radical and actually live out a life of excellence to its fullest degree. Remember, excellence exceeds expectations.

CHAPTER SEVEN: *Excellence - a Godly Process*

The Seven Beliefs of Excellence

After thinking about excellence for a number of years, I have composed a list that I call, "The Seven Beliefs of Excellence." These are seven beliefs to hold in your heart and when applied in your life will bring you to excellence.

1. A Belief in Being the Best

Do you believe you can be the best at whatever you are doing? Do you believe you can be the best mother? The best wife? The best father? The best husband? The best secretary? The best worker? The best neighbor? If you are saying no, you are probably comparing yourself with others and compiling an extensive list of your inadequacies. Stop doing that and be the best you can be. Start there. If you aim at nothing you are sure to hit it. It is far better to jump for the moon and reach the lamppost, then jump for the lamppost and not get off the ground. You need to believe that you can be the best.

> *"People will judge your ministry by the care you take of it."*

2. A Belief in Quality

I am talking about superior quality over cheaper costs. I remember attending a seminar twenty years ago and I noticed that the binders that they gave us were of excellent quality and the paper was a superior grade with texture. At the time, I remember thinking, "They have really done a good job in presenting their material." All these years later after much use of the binder, it still works and clicks open smoothly and the paper is unworn with no dog-ears. One of the principles that was shared at the seminar was, "People will judge your ministry by the care you take of it." The value of this truth is evident, that after all these years I am using them as an example. The leaders of the workshop did not just teach the principle of quality but practiced it. If we choose quality, our work will stand out. There will be a greater respect and appreciation given to what you say and do.

3. A Belief in the Importance of Planning

You need to have a plan. Now this is one belief that I had to personally work on. My natural make-up and tendency is to be unorganized and do things at the last minute. During high school, my natural ability allowed me to get by without putting in much effort. I would do projects at the last minute and cram for exams. I received good marks, but on the whole, not great marks. I could have done much better. It took a concerted effort on my part to break these bad habits. Now I desire to excel and not just "get by." I have learned that I can do an excellent job when I take the time to focus, plan, and prepare. We must never allow laziness to cause planning to fall by the wayside.

4. A Belief in the Importance of Teamwork

What we cannot do alone we can do together. The Bible tells us,

> *Two are better than one because they have a good reward for their labor. Though one may be overpowered by another, two can withstand him and a threefold cord is not quickly broken.*
> *Ecclesiastes 4:9,12*

It is important to draw a team around you. Whatever project you are working on, formally or informally, gather a group of people to help you. No matter how talented you are, you can benefit from the input of others. Each person brings a different perspective, talent and gifting that can add value. Gather people around you who have complementary gifts to yours. I used to prepare my Sunday messages on my own. Now, I have a team that gathers weekly to set the theme of the service and give advice and counsel on my message. Few things cannot be done better by working with a team.

> *Few things cannot be done better by working with a team.*

5. A Belief in the Importance of Details

Excellence is in the fine details. It is in the little things. A friend, who is a builder told me once, if you want to know the quality of construction in a house, look at how the trim work is done. Do the miter joints meet properly or are there gaps filled with caulking? Are the tops of the door sills painted or left because they are not seen? It is in the fine details that you can see whether something is excellent or not. Most people give attention to major items but little attention to that which is not seen or visible to others. As a pastor, I can have all the components of a service planned but not think about the transitions in a service. Where will the person stand when they come up to do their announcement, what microphone will they use, who will move the mic stand when necessary? All of these things seem small and insignificant but when done well, add excellence to the service.

6. A Belief in the Importance of Evaluation

Everything should be evaluated. This is a given in the business world. Did we meet our goal? What went well? What could have been done better? Is this still worth doing? What do we do differently now as a result? A company cannot maintain excellence without evaluation. What about you? Do you evaluate the critical areas of your life? How are you doing as a husband? A wife? A mother? A father? As a member of the church? You will never achieve excellence without honest evaluation.

> *You will never achieve excellence without honest evaluation.*

7. A Belief that Anything Can Be Improved
If you have done it once, you can do it better the second time. You can always improve on what you have done. The question is, "Will you put the time and effort into doing it?"

Let me share with you what happened a number of years ago when I first began to preach on this aspect of excellence in the church. I asked our volunteer youth leader, Larry, if he would have a different youth read Scripture in the Sunday service over the next five weeks. When I asked him to do this he said to me "You know, I have really enjoyed and benefitted from your teaching on excellence and I would like to have the young people read these Scriptures to excellence." Without thinking too much about it, I said, "For sure, go ahead and do that." Then he said, "You know I really want them to practice" and I said, "Good. I'll get you the Scripture references so they can practice at home." Then he said, "Oh no, I want them to practice here at the church. I'd like to have the sound person here as well, so they can practice reading into the microphone in front of the church. I want them to feel comfortable and do an excel-

CHAPTER SEVEN: *Excellence - a Godly Process*

lent job." I did not say it out loud, but I thought to myself, "Larry, you're carrying this a little too far. I will have to inconvenience the sound man. A mutual schedule has to be worked out. Is all this really necessary?" But I refrained from saying anything because I didn't want to quench his enthusiasm for excellence. So he set it all up and I came and sat in on one of the practice sessions. He had the young people go up to the mic and begin to read, and he would stop them and say, "Oh no, no, you're not close enough to the mic. Make sure you get a little closer." As they began to read, he would stop them again and say "You're looking down at the Bible too much. I really need you to memorize at least the first few verses. Go over the rest of the passage again and again until you basically have it in memory. You can still have the Bible to look down at from time to time, but mostly I want you to look out and make eye contact with the audience." He continued to train them, teaching them to look from one side of the auditorium to the other as they were reading. I was sitting at the back and thinking, "Oh Larry, you are carrying this way too far." But again I stifled my reaction and thought, "Let's just see how this all works out."

You can always improve on what you have done. The question is, "Will you put the time and effort into doing it?"

Well, let me tell you, the next five weeks were incredible! As each teen began to read, the whole congregation was struck with amazement. They read without one mistake, without one stumble! They read with feeling, emphasizing the appropriate words, lifting their heads, looking at the congregation. It was stunning! I could not believe how well they had done. During those weeks, I would hear over and over again at the door how impressed people were with the Bible reading. One visitor said to me, "I was just blown away with the way the young person read the Scriptures this morning."

Then it suddenly sank in; excellence really does distinguish when it is applied. If it had been left to me, even after preaching on excellence, I would not have gone to the effort Larry did. I had thought that he was going overboard. But Larry had caught the seven principles of excellence and had applied them. By putting in the time and effort, he had achieved incredible results that brought honour to God and excited the listeners.

Excellence versus Perfection

As we close this chapter, I want to clarify that we are striving for excellence not perfection. The pursuit of perfection will only delay and hinder your progress. Perfectionists over-analyze and are fearful to act, lest something is done imperfectly. This thinking chokes out creativity and innovation. Perfectionism waits while excellence acts. Excellence does the best it can do, right now, and seeks to improve the next time. It is amazing how a small improvement can result in success. Tiger Woods dominated the golf world for so long not because he was fifty percent better than other golfers, but because he was three or four percent better. Being just a few strokes better per round made him stand out among his peers.

Excellence is a part of God's L.I.F.E. that He has put within us. Let's draw upon it and do everything to the very best of our ability as unto the Lord.

CHAPTER
Eight

Living Out Your New Life

The unexamined life is not worth living.

- Socrates

We often hear the admonition to 'Keep your life in balance.' It usually refers to keeping all the different components of our life – family, work, friends, recreation – in the right proportion, giving each its proper time and importance. To keep balance, we are encouraged to prioritize them according to their relative value and then to adjust our life, spending more of our time on some and cutting back on others. This is all good, but in this book we have been sharing about a different kind of life – a L.I.F.E. that comes from God. Its four components – Love, Integrity, Forgiveness and Excellence – do not need to be balanced as they balance each other. A person can pursue each to the fullest degree without jeopardizing the others. When these four attributes first came to my mind I was unaware of just how well they balanced each other. It was only after sharing them and seeing their application over a number of years that I realized how beautifully they counterbalanced each other. None of them exist on their own, but fit together in a beautiful, symmetrical balance. Love balances excellence and integrity balances forgiveness.

> *Too often we have a poverty mentality that believes there is not enough to go around.*

Love and Excellence Balance

The definition of love is giving unselfishly to the needs of others without regard to personal recognition or reward. Love is the primary aspect of Christ's Life that He wants us to manifest. Its focus is on others and a desire for their good over our own. It is usually viewed as a sacrificial lifestyle but in reality it is not. It is only drawing upon God's Love within and releasing it through our lives, which in turn produces in us a feeling of great satisfaction. Jesus said,

> *There is more happiness in giving than in receiving.*
> Acts 20:35 (CJB)

The pleasure of giving is greater than any pleasure that acts of self-indulgence could produce on their own. However, there is still an inherent danger when love is pursued independently. We can be tempted to think that self-denial is valued by God and a worthwhile goal within itself. This kind of asceticism should be rejected. God takes no pleasure in His people having less because of their allegiance and obedience to Him. We are King's kids and God desires us to experience all the benefits of being His children. We need not avoid or apologize for the blessings that the Lord showers upon our lives.

Giving to the needs of others does not mean that our own needs, and even desires, cannot be met. Too often we have a poverty mentality that believes there is not enough to go around. We think that there is an insufficient supply to meet the needs of others and our own. We accept the premise that to meet the needs of others, we must suffer lack. But God is generous and has a vast supply, so we can love, put others first, give to their needs, and still expect and believe for an abundance in our own life. This is where excellence balances love. Excellence is a belief in having the best, and doing your best as unto the Lord.

When excellence is balanced by love you can focus on the needs of others first without losing faith for your own needs to be met in abundance.

God's Excellence desires that what you have is of the best quality, so that when God's Love prompts you to give to the needs of others, it is a gift of excellence. If you have two coats, the one you give is excellent and the one you keep for your own use is also excellent. If you only have one coat, God's Love may prompt you to give it freely without expecting anything in return. At the same time, God's Excellence will encourage you to work to the best of your ability for an even better coat for yourself in the future. The quality of excellence when pursued without the accompanying quality of love could lead to self-indulgence and materialism. But when excellence is balanced by love you can focus on the needs of others first without losing faith for your own needs to be met in abundance. God intends these two principles to work together, love balancing the principle of excellence, and excellence balancing the principle of love.

> *Forgiveness balances integrity, and integrity balances forgiveness.*

Integrity and Forgiveness Balance
The same balance applies to the aspects of integrity and forgiveness. Integrity is living up to all that you know and, when failing to do so, freely confessing to God and others where you fall short. Integrity will not permit any compromise with evil. It will not allow any tolerance for unethical or immoral behavior in your life. It will look beyond actions and shine a bright light to reveal the motives and intents of your heart. It will not abide the smallest trace of sin. Now if you only had the principle of integrity working within your life, you might be tempted to subject others around you to the same extensive scrutiny. If you do, you will become judgmental, comparing their behaviour with your own and determining where they come short. You may think, "They aren't living right. They need to do better. I'm lining up, why aren't they?" Jesus warns of this attitude and says,

> *Judge not, that you be not judged. For with what judgment you judge, you will be judged; and with the measure you use, it will be measured back to you. And why do you look at the speck in your brother's eye, but do not consider the plank in your own eye? Or how can you say to your brother, 'Let me remove the speck from your eye'; and look, a plank is in your own eye?*
>
> Matthew 7:1-4

Jesus says in this passage that we are to examine the plank in our own eye and not the speck in the other person's eye. In short, He says to focus on yourself and to not judge others.

> *Judge not, and you shall not be judged. Condemn not, and you shall not be condemned. Forgive, and you will be forgiven.*
>
> Luke 6:37

In this passage, Jesus again tells us not to judge or condemn, but then goes on to tell us what we should do. He tells us to forgive. It is this third aspect of Christ's L.I.F.E. that we are to extend to others.

Forgiveness is forgiving everybody, all the time, for everything, before they ask and before they change. If you have this attitude you cannot possibly be judgmental. You can and should learn from the mistakes of others for your own benefit, but you are not to assess blame and judgment on them. The scripture tells us that,

> *... the Lord does not see as man sees for man looks at the outward appearance, but the Lord looks at the heart.*
>
> 1 Samuel 16:7

We only see the outward actions of others but know nothing of their heart or inward motivations, so the Bible tells us not to judge. Paul concludes the same and writes,

> *Therefore, judge nothing before the time, until the Lord comes, who will both bring to light the hidden things of darkness and reveal the counsels of the hearts.*
> 1 Corinthians 4:5

We can judge ourselves because we can examine our own motives and intents, and the scripture encourages us to do so,

> *For if we would judge ourselves, we would not be judged.*
> 1 Corinthians 11:3

So we learn that it is essential that we judge ourselves. We do this by applying the principle of integrity and holding ourselves to a high standard without any compromise. However, in regards to others, we are to refrain from judging, and extend forgiveness in its place. Forgiveness balances integrity, and integrity balances forgiveness. If you only had the attitude of forgiveness, you would tend to become lax and give yourself freedom to do wrong, and your forgiveness of others could be interpreted as condoning their actions and a license to sin. But when you are living your own life in integrity, others see both the Godly standard that you are holding yourself to, and the forgiveness you receive from God and extend to others.

When you live with personal integrity, the forgiveness that you extend to others will not be misinterpreted as condoning their sin. Your forgiveness, however, will remove the feeling of judgment and condemnation from them. Condemnation will only cause them to harden their heart and become defensive and resistant. Forgiveness accompanied by personal integrity will produce conviction. Conviction opens their heart and allows God's power to transform them. This is a delicate balance we are exhorted to strive for. Paul writes,

> *Brethren, if a man is overtaken in any trespass, you who are spiritual restore such a one in a spirit of gentleness, considering yourself lest you also be tempted.*
>
> *Galatians 6:1*

Here we are told how we should act toward someone who has done wrong. First we are told that this is only for those who are spiritual.

When you live with personal integrity, the forgiveness that you extend to others will not be misinterpreted as condoning their sin.

People who are spiritually mature have grown in God's L.I.F.E. – embracing His Love, Integrity, Forgiveness and Excellence. It is a mark of spiritual maturity to maintain the balance of love and excellence, integrity and forgiveness. See how this is demonstrated in this portion of scripture. The person who attempts to restore someone must be spiritually mature – they have drawn upon God's Love to overcome their own personal hurt or loss, and are able to think of the offender's needs first. They go in a spirit of gentleness to restore the person and not just to expose their sin. They recognize that they too have been tempted and have needed forgiveness in the past. So they go with a clean heart of integrity while extending forgiveness and grace to the offender. These are the actions that will be the most effective in reaching people and seeing them restored.

Jesus expands our understanding of this in His teaching,

> *But I say to you, love your enemies, bless those who curse you, do good to those who hate you, and pray for those who spitefully use you and persecute you.*
>
> Matthew 5:44

Here Jesus teaches how a spiritually mature person responds to hurt and injury. It is just the opposite of what we would normally expect. The natural inclination of our own life is inadequate. The only way that we can follow the teaching of Christ is to do it in His L.I.F.E. We can love our enemies when we are secure in God's protection and provision. His Excellence provides this security. He is our source and will give us the best of all that we need. In this understanding, we can draw on God's Love and bless and speak well of those who offend us. We pray for them and ask God to forgive them. Then with love, integrity and forgiveness we do something good (excellent) for them. These are the balancing aspects of the Life of Christ within us.

Now that we have knowledge of these four aspects of Christ's L.I.F.E., what practical steps should we take to live them out? How do we apply them?

Jesus said that the blessing comes with the doing not with the knowing.

The Application

Doing a rough calculation, I was surprised to discover that I have preached over 6700 messages in the church that I pastor, and have given over 3000 talks on the radio. And if I may say so, the material that I shared was Biblical and compelling. You would think that I would be a spiritual giant by now, as well as all my listeners. But sadly that is not the case. It is one thing to know something and another to do it. Jesus said to His disciples after teaching them,

> *If you know these things, blessed are you if you do them.*
> *John 13:17*

It is important to note that Jesus said that the blessing comes with the doing not with the knowing. We can be deceived by thinking that we are mature by just knowing spiritual truths. Paul warns the Corinthian Christians of this very fact,

> *We know that we all have knowledge. Knowledge makes people arrogant, but love builds people up.*
> *1 Corinthians 8:1*

Knowledge will not benefit us unless it is applied to our lives. Jesus concluded His Sermon on the Mount, which laid out so many marvelous truths, by giving this illustration,

> *Therefore, whoever hears these sayings of Mine, and does them, I will liken him to a wise man who built his house on the rock: and the rain descended, the floods came, and the winds blew and beat on that house; and it did not fall, for it was founded on the rock. But everyone who hears these say-*

ings of Mine, and does not do them, will be like a foolish man who built his house on the sand: and the rain descended, the floods came, and the winds blew and beat on that house; and it fell. And great was its fall.

Matthew 7:24-27

I have heard these verses quoted many times in sermons but I have never personally heard them employed for the purpose Jesus did. Usually, they are used to say that we need to build our lives on the Rock, Christ Jesus, and if we do, our spiritual lives will never suffer loss; but if we build our lives on the sand of the world, then when the tests of life come, we will not stand. This of course is true, but this was not what Jesus was illustrating in this story. He said "whoever hears these sayings of Mine, and does them" was like the man who built his house on the rock, and "everyone who hears these sayings of Mine, and does not do them" was like the man who built his life upon the sand. The whole point of the illustration was to tell the people that they could hear His words, but unless they applied them, it would do them no good.

Application is of vital importance to live out Christ's L.I.F.E.

Application is of vital importance to live out Christ's L.I.F.E. We are not the source of these attributes; they must stem from the Life of Christ within. We do have a part to play in how clearly they come through our lives and are manifested. I want to be very prac-

CHAPTER EIGHT: *Living out your New L.I.F.E.*

tical here and give you some exercises that will help you to focus on doing your part.

Get a tablet, either paper or digital, and make a category on the top of each page – Love, Integrity, Forgiveness and Excellence.

LOVE

At the top of the first page or file write LOVE. Make a list of all the people in your family or life who are the closest to you and then for each one make a template similar to the one below.

Δ Name _____

◊ Aspects of their Lives

– Determine a Time and Place you will pray for them

1. Their Spiritual Life

  a) Their Goals and Needs

  _____
  _____
  _____

• Words from you that would encourage them

  _____
  _____

• Actions that would benefit them and lead to their success _____

  _____
  _____

2. Their Relationships
   a) Their Goals and Needs

   _____

   _____

   _____

   - Words from you that would encourage them

     _____

     _____

   - Actions that would benefit them and lead to their success _____

     _____

     _____

3. Their Workplace
   a) Their Goals and Needs

   _____

   _____

   _____

   - Words from you that would encourage them

     _____

     _____

   - Actions that would benefit them and lead to their success _____

     _____

     _____

4. Their Finances
   a) Their Goals and Needs

   _____

   _____

   • Words from you that would encourage them

   _____

   _____

   • Actions that would benefit them and lead to their success _____

   _____

Following the same template make a list of names for "Neighbours and Friends" and "Work Associates." Now, go even further and make lists under "People Who Irritate Me" and "People I Have Conflict With." Remember Jesus taught that we should love our enemies. If you want to experience God's Love shining through you, you need to intentionally express it in practical ways. You do not need to feel like doing it – remember it is not your love – we just need to initiate God's Love and He will provide the power for you to follow through.

*We just need to initiate God's Love
and He will provide the power for you
to follow through.*

INTEGRITY

At the top of the second page or file write INTEGRITY.
On this page write down all the areas you are falling short in, things you know God wants you to be or do, but you are not fulfilling. Make a template similar to the one below.

∆ List Aspects of your Life

1. **Personal**
    ◊ List Areas of Sin or Lack of Integrity
    (Pray and ask God to search your heart)

    _____

    _____

    _____

    o List the Actions that You Will Take to Restore your Integrity

    _____

    _____

    _____

2. **Your Workplace**
    ◊ List Areas of Sin or Lack of Integrity
    (Pray and ask God to search your heart)

    _____

    _____

    _____

CHAPTER EIGHT: *Living out your New L.I.F.E.*

o List the Actions that You Will Take to Restore your Integrity

_____
_____
_____

3. Your Finances
◊ List Areas of Sin or Lack of Integrity
(Pray and ask God to search your heart)

_____
_____
_____

o List the Actions that You Will Take to Restore your Integrity

_____
_____
_____

4. Your Relationships
◊ List Areas of Sin or Lack of Integrity
(Pray and ask God to search your heart)

_____
_____
_____

o List the Actions that You Will Take to Restore your Integrity

_____

_____

_____

To maintain your integrity, it is important that you have people who will come along side and strengthen you.
- Establish a relationship with an accountability partner
- Set a schedule to meet regularly
- Confess your sins
- Share your strongest temptations
- Ask him or her to share with you any blind spots that you may have

Keep short tabs on the hurts of life.

FORGIVENESS

On the third page or file write FORGIVENESS. Make a template similar to the one below.

Δ Name _____

   (List names of people who have hurt you in the past)

◊ List the hurt _____

   (Ask God to forgive them, and choose to forgive them yourself)

      o **Actions you can take**
- Time and Place you will pray for this person

  _____

- Ask God what character trait He is developing in you through this experience

  _____

- Determine how and when you will "do good" to this person

  _____

The people you need to forgive are the people who have hurt you in some way. This process is very hard to do without seeing your offender through God's eyes and drawing on His Love and Forgiveness for the individual. This exercise is one you should practice regularly in prayer. Keep short tabs on the hurts of life. The little seed of hurt sprouts resentment. Resentment turns into the stalk of bitterness. Bitterness eventually bears the fruit of hate.

You need to ask for God's forgiveness to come in and cut down this plant in your life before it bears its fruit. You start by realizing that nothing happens to you by chance without God knowing, and that He will work it for good in your life in some way. Pray that people who have offended you don't get what they deserve. Then pray for them and do something good for them.

The goal is to raise the standard of excellence in every area of your life.

CHAPTER EIGHT: *Living out your New L.I.F.E.*

EXCELLENCE

Finally, on the last page or file write EXCELLENCE. Make a template similar to the one below.

Δ Aspects of your Life

1. Your Personal Life
   - ◊ Rate how you are doing in your personal life on a scale of 1 – 10. _____

   - ◊ What one thing can you do to improve and move up the scale? _____

   - ◊ Who can help you with this and hold you accountable?
   _____

2. Your Possessions
   - ◊ Rate how you are doing with your possessions on a scale of 1 – 10. _____

   - ◊ What one thing can you do to improve and move up the scale? _____

   - ◊ Who can help you with this and hold you accountable?
   _____

3. Your Workplace
   - ◊ Rate how you are doing with your work on a scale of 1 – 10. _____

◊ What one thing can you do to improve and move
  up the scale? _____

◊ Who can help you with this and hold you accountable?
_____

4. Your Projects
◊ Rate how you are doing in completing your projects
  on a scale of 1 – 10. _____

◊ Establish a plan with goals and steps of action
  for each project. _____

  o Set a schedule with deadlines to your steps.
  _____

  o As much as possible enlist others to help you
    and hold you accountable.
  _____

◊ Who can help you with this and hold you accountable?
_____

The goal is to raise the standard of excellence in every area of your life. It applies to all you possess and everything that you do. Be sure that the motivation for improvement is a desire to keep everything, and to do everything, as unto the Lord, for His glory and honour. Be conscious that as you do, the most insignificant task that you do in life can be elevated to an expression of worship, and become eligible for an eternal reward.

CHAPTER EIGHT: *Living out your New L.I.F.E.*

Putting It All Together

We started this book with the words of Jesus, "I have come that you may have life, and that you may have it more abundantly."[38] The central reality of becoming a Christian is that your spirit that was dead and dormant is regenerated by receiving the Life of Christ. This infusion of God's Spirit empowers you to experience life at a whole new level. The contrast is like going from a black and white world to one of full colour. Not only does God want you to enjoy this new Life, but He wants you to manifest it to others. You are the prism that shines forth the full colour spectrum of God's Life to the world.

We have seen how God's L.I.F.E. includes four primary attributes – Love, Integrity, Forgiveness and Excellence which are expressed to the world in the following ways:

- Godly Love is manifested by giving unselfishly to the needs of others without desiring personal recognition or reward.

- Godly Integrity is manifested by living up to all that you know and, when failing to do so, freely confessing to God and others where you fall short.

- Godly Forgiveness is manifested by forgiving everybody, all the time, for everything before they ask, and before they change.

- Godly Excellence is manifested by caring for everything and doing everything to the very best of your ability, as though you were doing it for God.

---

38. John 10;10

These attributes of God are beyond our natural capability to produce and can only be expressed by cooperating and yielding to the Spirit of God. The more we understand the nature of these components of God's L.I.F.E. the more we can work with Him in expressing them. As we do so, we begin to figure out why we go through the things that we do. We discover that the difficult times in our life are utilized by God to showcase His attributes. God never wastes a hurt. As we embrace this understanding, we attach new meaning to the things we face and begin to react differently. Our attitude changes and we become more concerned about our reaction in a situation than the situation itself. When we are called upon to sacrifice to meet the needs of others, we no longer feel imposed upon, but rather welcome it as an opportunity to show God's Love.

> *You are the prism that shines forth the full colour spectrum of God's Life to the world.*

When people treat us unfairly and offend us with their words and actions, we no longer feel beaten down and injured, but rather take it as an opening to express God's forgiveness. Not only does this benefit the other person but it benefits us as well. It frees us from self-pity and bitterness and prompts change in the one who has wronged us. As we experience God's Integrity, we take off our masks and become authentic and comfortable in our own skin. Realizing that God accepts us just the way we are, we are unafraid to confess our faults to Him, and ask forgiveness of those around us. This honesty and openness frees us from guilt and provides an

CHAPTER EIGHT: *Living out your New L.I.F.E.*

inner peace. Pursuing excellence for God's glory gives meaning to our lives and encourages us to reach our full potential. We find ourselves on an ever improving journey through life that brings glory to God and inspires the people around us. Receiving Christ certainly gives us an abundant life!

> *When we are called upon to sacrifice, welcome it as an opportunity to show God's Love.*

However, sometimes our concept of abundant life is so broad and encompassing that it seems overwhelming. We are uncertain where to focus and how to practically engage. But I trust that your understanding is clearer now, and you see that the Life of Christ can be simplified to the four fundamental aspects of Love, Integrity, Forgiveness and Excellence. My prayer for you is that you will pursue these attributes with new faith and knowledge, and experience their reality. This participation with God to show forth His Life is freeing and exhilarating. It fulfills your deepest desires and accomplishes God's purpose. This is what you were created for and nothing else can give you as much lasting joy, pleasure and satisfaction. This new L.I.F.E. is what Jesus promised and it is certainly worth living!

Now, go forward and enjoy!

Appreciation

My special thanks goes to the following people:

To Josh Gordon who first encouraged me to write this book and guided the process from start to finish.

To Stephanie Steffler, Beth Schilling and my wife, Kay for their practical suggestions in editing and proof-reading the manuscript.

To David Nikolic who facilitated the production of the book.

Made in the USA
Columbia, SC
24 February 2024